Joy In Surrender

Joy In Surrender

DEBORAH STRICKLIN

BL BRIDGE
LOGOS

Newberry, FL 32669

Bridge-Logos

Newberry, FL 32669

Joy in Surrender: Living a Life Yielded to God

by Deborah Rae Stricklin

Printed in the United States of America.

Library of Congress Catalog Card Number: 2018949503

International Standard Book Number: 9781610362153

Literary Agent and Editor:
L. Edward Hazelbaker
11907 S. Sangre Road
Perkins, OK 74059
E-mail: l.edward@thewornkeyboard.com

Cover/interior design: Kent Jensen | knail.com

Dedication

My thanks to the following cheerleaders in my life—encouragers who celebrate with me and help me become better at what I do. Their timely words of encouragement keep me moving forward in the face of life's obstacles.

My husband, friends, parents, and pastors. And my children, who especially amaze me with their continual uplifting words and actions.

Kirsten, my first-born, who provides me with an ever-present smile and the constant challenge, "So what's stopping you from doing *that*, Mom?" I always walk away from our conversations believing that the next step in my journey is possible.

Heather, my child who is most like me in personality (and appearance), and who joins me in my lifelong dedication to excellence. She notices every detail, even seeing what I sometimes miss; I'm grateful.

Jonathon, my son, who is known as a man of few words. With perfect timing, his dry humor or a well-chosen *attaboy* draws out from me an irrepressible smile.

And my sons-in-law, Jordan and Seth, who have only added to my joy in parenting. They both are the blessing of new life breathed into our family.

And finally, my literary agent and editor, L. Edward Hazelbaker, who has truly made this manuscript better than it could have been without his help. He challenged me, pushed me, and stretched me into new growth in my writing. Thank you, Lynn, for closing the gaps in this manuscript and helping me discover more of the potential inside of me.

—DS

Foreword

I'd love to be able to swim, but I can't. I've taken lessons from an Olympic swimmer. I've even purchased swimming gear including fins for my feet. I took swimming lessons for weeks. But I finally gave up.

I couldn't surrender. I couldn't surrender to the water.

I couldn't surrender control.

Today I watch my children and grandchildren swim like fish. I love to watch them having fun, but I must admit I wish so badly that I could swim with them.

Surrender is not necessarily a sign of weakness. It can be a strength. Surrendering my life, my plans, and my preferences to Jesus result in what the author of this book aptly titled *Joy in Surrender*.

Surrendering selfishness enhances a marriage. Surrendering unforgiveness leads to a healthier life. Surrendering dogmatism will unfold new horizons in relationships. Surrendering our finances to the Lord brings heavenly abundance. And surrendering to His will saves us from unnecessary heartaches and detours in life.

Deborah Stricklin constructs a masterful exposition of Peter's life—his life learnings, heartaches, teaching, struggles, and admonitions extracted from his first letter. You will find the author's transparency refreshing and her biblical applications relevant to our lives today.

Surrender—there is *Joy in Surrender*.

—Dr. Samuel R. Chand
AUTHOR, FOUNDER AND PRESIDENT OF DREAM RELEASER COACHING,
AND PRESIDENT EMERITUS OF BEULAH HEIGHTS UNIVERSITY

Table of Contents

Introduction

The pain and anguish of suffering can cause us to lose hope. This can especially be true when we are persecuted or when our faith is being challenged in other significant ways. First-century followers of Christ understood that. They were being brutally persecuted, and many were forced to leave their homes. They were scattered in foreign countries, and because of the persecution they experienced, the temptation some felt to lose hope and turn back from their faith was very real.

I am using the life of Peter and his words written in the first epistle of Peter as the springboard for writing this book. Peter showed great concern for those who were suffering persecution. Peter was able to minister to them and encourage them with authority and compassion. And that was at least partly due to the fact that Peter himself knew temptation, failure, and persecution from firsthand experience. And he knew the suffering those things brought.

Peter knew suffering, but he also knew his Lord. Nothing could unseat his confidence in the risen Christ. In his first letter (the first epistle of Peter) he addressed scattered, suffering believers, and he encouraged them to hold tightly to their faith, live holy lives, and stand firmly on the *living Cornerstone*,[1] Jesus Christ.

Peter's words of instruction and encouragement continue to apply to us today. He pointed believers toward Jesus to find the strength to persevere. And in the midst of our own suffering, it is still Christ—who himself overcame temptation, lived His life in obedience to His Heavenly Father, and was rejected and killed—who serves as our ultimate example of how we can faithfully obey and serve God through suffering and sacrifice.

Using vivid imagery, Peter painted a picture of the hope and joy that is ours as we surrender our lives to the faithful One we call our Savior and Lord. Peter used the imagery of the Temple and its priestly service in the letter to remind believers that they were part of a larger, beautiful whole. Then he reminded them of how, like lost sheep, they had turned to their *Shepherd*, the *Guardian* of their souls.[2]

And now Peter's words to those first-century Christians, and Peter's own experience as a follower of Jesus, encourage

---

1   "You are coming to Christ, who is the living cornerstone of God's temple. He was rejected by people, but he was chosen by God for great honor" (1 Peter 2:4).

2   1 Peter 2:25.

us to find the joy that is available to only those who fully yield to that same *Great Shepherd* [3] and commit themselves to remaining engaged in living out His plan for their lives under His compassionate care.

—Deborah

---

3 "And when the Great Shepherd appears, you will receive a crown of never-ending glory and honor" (1 Peter 5:4).

CHAPTER 1

Called Forth in Faith

YOU AND I are being called forth in faith.

Although a lot of people readily agree with this statement, there are many who do not fully understand its implications or the challenges it can present to us. And there are yet others who are not even ready to entertain the call—and perhaps they barely hear it—because they are struggling with the entire notion of faith and what it means to their lives.

"But what is faith?" some ask.

Faith to many seems like such an intangible concept. Yet as Christians we know that faith is not only tangible (it can be recognized and understood), it is something we need a firm grasp on; for the entirety of who we are and what we are to become is built upon it.

James tells us that faith can be seen and understood through our works—our actions.[4] And as translated in the New King James Version, the writer of Hebrews provides a short definition of faith at the beginning of the eleventh chapter by stating it is *"the substance of things hoped for, the evidence of things not seen."*[5] Then, in his next sentence, he further clarifies for his readers what faith is and how it operates. The New Living Translation of the Bible puts together both statements this way:

> *Faith is the confidence that what we hope for will actually happen; it gives us assurance about things we cannot see. Through their faith, the people in days of old earned a good reputation.* (Hebrews 11:1-2)[6]

The writer of Hebrews clearly understood that faith cannot be fully explained in a simple sentence. So he continued throughout the eleventh chapter to further define it—to demonstrate how faith is to be recognized and understood through those who have it. Faith can be both seen and understood through our actions.

Faith is real, and the way we demonstrate it affects our lives. It is "substance." It is "evidence." And having it brings "confidence" and "assurance."

---

4 James 2:14-25.
5 Hebrews 11:1 (NKJV).
6 Holy Bible, New Living Translation ®, copyright © 1996, 2004 by Tyndale Charitable Trust. Used by permission of Tyndale House Publishers. All rights reserved.

At least that is what *faith* does for Christians.

People can put their faith and confidence in many things. Some people put their faith in Humanism—a system of belief that attaches primary significance to human intelligence and understanding. This openly facilitates the worship of man over God.

Some people place their faith in the teachings of evolution; they trust in their belief that it is nature, not God, who is worthy of honor. And for thousands of years people around the world have invented and fashioned idols to represent gods birthed out of their own imaginations and human reasoning. They foolishly place their faith and trust in "gods" made by human hands—gods who have no power to save them.[7]

It's difficult for many people to move beyond what they know and understand in the physical world. When they begin to deal with spiritual things they often get caught up in building their concepts of God based on their own earthly terms. They would rather trust in things they can touch. They have trouble turning toward Christ and accepting Him as their Savior because doing so requires them to place their faith in a God they cannot see.

---

7   "It is true, LORD, that the kings of Assyria have destroyed all these nations. And they have thrown the gods of these nations into the fire and burned them. But of course the Assyrians could destroy them! They were not gods at all—only idols of wood and stone shaped by human hands" (Isaiah 37:18-19).

However, even for Christians—those who have already come to Christ in faith—maintaining our faith can sometimes be challenging. Learning to walk with Jesus through the difficulties, emotions, and hardships that we confront in life challenges us. But if we are handling our challenges properly, the things we experience continue to move us toward understanding more about, and leaning into, this thing called faith.

The truth is, even people who struggle to understand this concept we know as *faith* are actually always demonstrating some form of faith and putting their trust in things beyond themselves. They trust in various beliefs and theories, and by doing so they are placing their trust in those things to bring meaning to their lives on earth and in the *hereafter*.

It does not take a brilliant person to figure out that all opinions on what is true cannot be right. We understand as followers of Christ that we must not only accurately understand truth but also live it out. And the ultimate source of truth is the Word of God. We must apply ourselves to digging out Scriptural truths, and then we must follow them.

Since we are unable to dismiss ourselves from the concept of placing faith somewhere, or in something, there are some logical questions we all must answer:

In what do we place our faith? And if we're talking about pleasing and following a deity or spiritual leadership, in whom do we profess our faith? This was the crux of the matter when Jesus asked His followers a question one day in the city of Caesarea Philippi.

Caesarea Philippi was a city of ancient origin located at the southwestern base of Mount Hermon. Mount Hermon sits on the border between Syria and Lebanon, and it is situated within the Golan Heights now occupied by Israel. In the times of Jesus it had been rebuilt by Philip the Tetrarch, son of King Herod I. The Roman emperor Tiberius Caesar made Philip the ruler of that region, and Philip maintained his capitol there until 33 AD.

One of Jesus' disciples, Matthew, recorded the question Jesus asked that day. According to Matthew, they were just entering Caesarea Philippi when Jesus asked them, *"Who do people say that I, the Son of Man am?"* [8]

Jesus wasn't looking for personal affirmation with that question. He didn't need it. He asked the question to make a carefully crafted point for His disciples. That question started a conversation in which He challenged His disciples to clarify their own faith.

Christ's disciples offered their answers. Crowds of people had watched Jesus perform miracles, righteously confront the religious hierarchy, and show unrequited love toward

8   Matthew 16:13 (NKJV).

a rebellious people; and they had various opinions. The disciples told Jesus that some people thought He was John the Baptist (come back from the dead) or Elijah (who was taken to heaven in a whirlwind without dying). They told Jesus that others said He was Jeremiah or one of the other prophets (whose spirit had returned).

After receiving their answers, Jesus masterfully led His closest followers to His next question: *"But who do you say I am?"* [9]

It's easy to offer an answer when our answers don't convey personal significance, but it's sometimes more difficult to offer answers when we are called upon to examine our own understanding of things. Jesus wanted to get to the heart of the matter. He was looking for a heartfelt, verbal confession from those who had most closely witnessed His life.

Matthew records that it was Simon Peter who answered Jesus' second question. He said, *"You are the Messiah, the Son of the living God."* [10]

Perhaps there was a hesitation among the other disciples as they considered the proper response to give to Jesus. However, given Peter's bold personality, he likely answered quickly. But regardless, Peter's words came from his innermost being, and Jesus' reply to Peter's answer confirmed the Lord's approval of Peter's profound statement:

---

9   Matthew 16:15.
10 Matthew 16:16.

You are blessed, Simon son of John, because my Father in heaven has revealed this to you. You did not learn this from any human being. Now I say to you that you are Peter (which means "rock"), and upon this rock I will build my church, and all the powers of hell will not conquer it. And I will give you the keys of the Kingdom of Heaven. Whatever you forbid on earth will be forbidden in heaven, and whatever you permit on earth will be permitted in heaven. (Matthew 16:17-19)

Peter's confession that Jesus is the Son of God, the long-awaited Messiah, contained his words of faith. And just as Peter verbalized *his* belief, we too must do the same; and in doing so, we proclaim that the very foundation of our faith is our own confession that Jesus is the Christ. But let's focus on Peter's confession and the surrounding circumstances a while longer to consider what made that specific incident with Peter that day so significant.

Caesarea Philippi was a region where pagan temples and idols abounded. Sin ran rampant—providing a stark contrast to many other communities Jesus and His disciples visited. Yet Jesus brought His disciples to that sin-filled place to deliver powerful truths about the Kingdom of God. Jesus openly acknowledged himself to His disciples as Messiah there. And it was there where He let them know that His church was going to be built upon the truth of Peter's confession.

All the powers of hell could certainly be, at least in part, illustrated by the pagan worship around them there in Caesarea Philippi. Jesus made it clear that nothing would be able to stop what God himself was about to do. And we know that Peter, the first to answer and proclaim his faith in Christ so boldly, would soon serve as a great leader in the Church.

Peter's understanding of Christ's words spoken that day about the construction of His church grew in the coming years. And his understanding of that as well as Peter's maturity in ministry are reflected in the book he penned more than thirty years later:[11]

> *You are coming to Christ, who is the living cornerstone of God's temple. He was rejected by people, but he was chosen by God for great honor. And you are living stones that God is building into his spiritual temple. What's more, you are his holy priests. Through the mediation of Jesus Christ, you offer spiritual sacrifices that please God. As the Scriptures say, "I am placing a cornerstone in Jerusalem, chosen for great honor, and anyone who trusts in him will never be disgraced."* [12]   (1 Peter 2:4-6)

---

11 Many Bible scholars believe Peter wrote the first epistle of Peter between 64 and 68 AD.

12 "Therefore, this is what the Sovereign LORD says: 'Look! I am placing a foundation stone in Jerusalem, a firm and tested stone. It is a precious cornerstone that is safe to build on. Whoever believes need never be shaken'" (Isaiah 28:16).

Much happened in Peter's life during those thirty years between his initial confession and the seasoned, challenging words recorded in First Peter. Similar to our own experiences, Peter's growth in those intervening years had to have come at least in part from moments of painful self-awareness.

We sometimes see Peter before the Resurrection of Jesus and the Day of Pentecost as impetuous and over-confident. And his misplaced confidence in his own strength and abilities sometimes got him in trouble. When Peter failed, he, like us, was surely tempted to see himself through the lens of his missteps and painfully broken life.

Just as we may have our own temptations to *throw in the towel* in times of trouble and conflict, perhaps Peter too was tempted to become disappointed and give up—stop trying to be the person he knew he should be. But he knew he had been called by God, and surely the precious words of hope spoken to him by Jesus became a great catalyst for change in his life.

Probably one of the most impactful statements made by anyone in Peter's life was Jesus' declaration to him when Jesus first called him to be His disciple. Jesus told him, *"Your name is Simon, son of John—but you will be called Cephas' (which means "Peter")."*[13] The name *Peter* in Greek means a rock. This statement, pregnant with prophetic prediction, served as a defining reality for the rest of Peter's life.

---

13 John 1:42.

Before Jesus' death and resurrection, Simon Peter vacillated between his impetuous, unstable self (Simon) and the solid rock (Peter) that Jesus proclaimed him to be. In the gospels, we read that Peter walked on water at Jesus' bidding but then faltered and began to sink in fear.[14]

Then when Jesus began making it plain to His disciples that He was going to suffer in Jerusalem, be killed, and be resurrected, it was Peter who so boldly and self-confidently took Jesus aside to reprimand Him for saying such things.[15] Following that, as Peter witnessed Jesus' transfiguration when Moses and Elijah appeared on the mountain with Jesus, it was Peter who foolishly offered to build a memorial for each of them to commemorate the event.[16]

Then at the last Passover meal that Jesus shared with the disciples before His crucifixion, Peter proudly proclaimed that he was willing to go to prison and even suffer death with Jesus. In his attempt to protect Jesus in the Garden of Gethsemane, Peter showed courage when he drew his sword and cut off the ear of the high priest's servant.[17] But later, when the pressure was really on, Peter did exactly what Jesus said he would do: Peter denied three times that he even knew Jesus.[18]

---

14 Matthew 14:25-31.
15 Matthew 16:21-23.
16 Mark 9:2-8.
17 Mark 14:43-50.
18 Luke 22:31-34; Luke 22:54-62.

However, as we read in the book of Acts, Peter (the rock) preached boldly to crowds of thousands after being filled with the Holy Spirit on the Day of Pentecost. Later he laid his hands on the sick in the power of Jesus Christ and saw them healed. He defended Christ before the authorities. He was jailed for his faith but then freed by the angel of the Lord.[19]

Peter came to rejoice in suffering dishonor for the name of Jesus.

God used Peter to raise people from the dead.[20] And it was Peter whom the Lord called to courageously take the gospel to the Gentiles.[21] Peter's rocky start as Jesus' disciple yielded to a fruitful life that greatly impacted the Kingdom of God. Peter was far from perfect, but his moldable heart made him a candidate to be used by Jesus as He ushered in His Kingdom. Peter became a leader and man of great faith.

Peter was called forth in faith. He was given the opportunity to die to self and serve God effectively.[22] And like Peter, we also have the opportunity to be used mightily by the Lord; but our faith and trust in God, and the willingness of our hearts to follow Him in obedience, make all the difference in our effectiveness.

---

19 Acts 12:3–11.

20 Acts 9:36–42.

21 Acts 10.

22 "Then Jesus said to his disciples, 'If any of you wants to be my follower, you must give up your own way, take up your cross, and follow me. If you try to hang on to your life, you will lose it. But if you give up your life for my sake, you will save it'" (Matthew 16:24-25).

And like Peter, we too are called forth to leave behind our mistakes and failures in order to pursue the new life God has planned for us. Jesus set before Peter a new name, a name that anticipated someone Peter had not yet become. I'm grateful God sees us as we can be, not just as we are.

I often ask my teacher-education college students, "As a middle-schooler, did any of you know who you'd be as adults?"

The unanimous response by my students is always, "Not even close!"

Our view of ourselves is so limited, and we can't seem to stand far enough back to gain a new perspective. That's what makes God's vantage point so valuable; He sees the potential in us, even when we are still *yet to become.*

There is another "name" story in the Bible that fascinates me. It is the story in the book of Isaiah about the pagan king named *Cyrus.* He was the ruler who conquered the Babylonian empire and eventually set free the people of Israel—allowing them to return to their homeland. He was Cyrus II, Cyrus the Great, king of Persia.

When the armies of Cyrus conquered the Babylonians, Cyrus had no idea that he was doing God's bidding. But the Lord's call upon him, and his response to God, makes this story from history absolutely amazing. God predicted the events through His prophet, Isaiah, over a century before they happened.

Some scholars say that after Cyrus came to power in Babylon, he read the following passage written by Isaiah and was so moved by it that he carried out its words. Let's read Isaiah's impactful prediction of this man named *Cyrus*:

> *This is what the LORD says to Cyrus, his anointed one, whose right hand he will empower. Before him, mighty kings will be paralyzed with fear. Their fortress gates will be opened, never to shut again. This is what the LORD says: "I will go before you, Cyrus, and level the mountains. I will smash down gates of bronze and cut through bars of iron. And I will give you treasures hidden in the darkness—secret riches. I will do this so you may know that I am the LORD, the God of Israel,* **the one who calls you by name.**

> *"And why have I called you for this work?* **Why did I call you by name when you did not know me?** *It is for the sake of Jacob my servant, Israel my chosen one. I am the LORD; there is no other God. I have equipped you for battle, though you don't even know me, so all the world from east to west will know there is no other God. I am the LORD, and there is no other . . . I will raise up Cyrus to fulfill my righteous purpose, and I will guide his actions.*

He will restore my city and free my captive people—
without seeking a reward! I, the LORD of Heaven's Armies,
have spoken!"   (Isaiah 45:1-6, 13) [emphasis mine]

How incredible! God called Cyrus by name and outlined his purpose over a century before Cyrus was born.

But, let's make this personal. What if God had written down *your* name and His purpose for *your* life long before *you* were conceived? Would you be convinced after reading it that your life was ordained by God? Would you be convinced that you are both desired and valued? God's writing journal may not look like ours, but rest assured, He did record your name and purpose long before you entered the world.

Jeremiah, a powerful Old Testament prophet, wrote these words:

The LORD gave me a message: "I knew you before I formed
you in your mother's womb. Before you were born I set you
apart and appointed you as my prophet to the nations."

(Jeremiah 1:4-5)

How beautiful! God shows no favoritism.[23] If He knew Cyrus and Jeremiah before they were born, He knew you.[24] You are truly wanted; you are loved! And God has both a purpose and a plan for you. We are being called forth to

---

23 Acts 10:34.
24 See also David's words in Psalm 139:13.

fulfill God's plans for us, and He is waiting for us to press into Him and discover them.

With the biblical Old Testament judge and leader in mind, my parents purposefully named me Deborah.[25] Growing up, I was *Debbie*. The only time I heard my given name was when my actions called for immediate response: "Deborah Rae, come here!"

That happened more often than my quiet demeanor would suggest! I was a rather shy child, preferring to play by myself most of the time. Onlookers would never know it, but I had a playmate; I talked to Jesus like He was my closest friend. His words to me were always pleasant and right. Even as a child, I loved His written Word. I still remember my red, hard-backed Bible. By the time I had to get a new one, the worn-out pages of that Bible were barely clinging to its binding.

I carefully turned its pages as I read with great expectation. The seeds of my future were quietly being deposited through the words of my Savior. Over the years I somehow knew there was latent purpose inside me that wasn't yet ready to germinate, but there it lay for more than four decades like an unplanted seed with enormous potential. Through

25 Judges 4:4-5:31.

raising my children and growing in ministry, I began seeing glimpses of something powerfully familiar, but untapped.

The tumultuous waters of the last seven years of my life became the soil God finally used to cause that seed to sprout. Through painful tests of trust, patience, love, and endurance, God stretched me to maturity. And through times of great difficulty, I have begun to emerge as Deborah, the woman my parents envisioned the day they named their baby girl. Much like with Peter, Cyrus, and Jeremiah, God spoke my future long before I learned to walk in His purposes for my life.

You may be thinking your name doesn't mean anything spiritually significant, or that your parents put no great forethought into your arrival or your name. But, that doesn't disqualify you from the purpose-filled future *God* planned for you long ago! God is looking for those who will believe Him. He is searching out His children who will respond to Him with faith.

Believing God birthed us with purpose is foundational for us to move forward in faith. The sixth verse of Hebrews chapter eleven reminds us that *"it is impossible to please God without faith."* Looking around us, we see many people who seem to be satisfied with less than vibrant, faith-filled lives. Does this please God?

Lack of passionate living can become our standard if we're not watchful. God didn't call us to live passionless lives; He called us to boldly and adventurously follow His Holy Spirit.

Just because we have acknowledged God or accepted God's gracious gift of salvation doesn't mean we've learned to trust Him in leading us day by day. The faith to do that comes from a growing relationship based on a decidedly childlike trust in His ability to carry us through every circumstance.

Having grown up in the Tabernacle at Shiloh, Samuel walked in simple faith, gaining favor with both God and people.[26] In a time when messages from the Lord were very rare, Samuel, still a young child, heard the Lord's voice calling him, and he responded. Samuel too was being called forth in faith.

Since Eli, the High Priest and Samuel's guardian, was older, more experienced, and held the position that presumably entitled him to hear from God, we would expect the Lord to call out to Eli and talk to him about His plans for Samuel. But God chose to speak personally to Samuel. Perhaps it was because Samuel's faith was pure and unassuming. The long view of Samuel's life proved that his faith was worthy of God's attention and blessing.

---

26 1 Samuel 2:26.

Faith activates the potential inside us. This isn't some lofty, ethereal faith that we construct; this is faith that comes from reading the Word of God, accepting it as truth, and acting upon what it says.

Here is one of my favorite quotes. It has been attributed by several people to Dr. Lilian B. Yeomans:

> God delights in His children stepping out over the aching void with nothing underneath their feet but the Word of God. [27]

There's nothing easy about walking by faith. In concept it's simple, but it's not easy. As a matter of fact, it's easier to leave faith's seed of potential lying dormant inside us. Once the seed is awakened, the stages of faith's germination and its growth require activity on our part.

As a seed is planted in good soil, the seed absorbs water, and that activates growth proteins. It becomes so swollen with its potential for success that the seed coat splits, giving way to its new life. Roots shoot out of the seed looking for more sources of water to nourish the developing plant.

Still enveloped by darkness, the plant's stem emerges from the seed and seeks out a pathway upward through the soil to find sunlight to fuel its growth. The roots deepen, and after emerging from the soil, the plant grows larger and stronger as it stretches toward the light that promises

---

27 The original source is unknown.

to give it hope for its fruitful purpose. Moving from seed to productive plant involves a lot of work, but eventually it becomes worth all the effort.

When applied to our lives, no part of a seed's process of germination and struggle to emerge from darkness seems desirable. Growth is painful, but we'll never reach our destiny through our comfort. Unlike the seed, though, the choice to either allow our potential to remain dormant or accept it and live in faith is totally ours.

Our decision to respond to God's call and His plan for our lives is ours to make. We choose whether we're willing to accept our potential, whether we're willing to be stretched day after day, and whether we're willing to yield to the process inside us that brings about Christian maturity and spiritual growth.

Jesus is asking us, "Will you unlock the hold you have on your life so I can be loosed to birth *my* dreams for you?" Your permission grants Him access to the most deeply buried parts of your being. Only there can the process of what God wants to do in your life begin.

Whether potential needs to be called forth from your life, or you need the fresh start of accepting a new name that the Lord may want to give you, God is in the business of new beginnings. Metaphorically, or even literally if God desires, let Him rename you.

Perhaps sickness or an accident has left you with a new

set of challenges; let God call forth His plans for this season of your life. Divorce or the death of a loved one may have left you feeling like you are less than a whole person; let God fill the void that you feel and launch you on a new trajectory. Maybe your own bad decisions have rendered you paralyzed in your expectations of being able to change your future; know that God isn't finished with you yet.

None of us are exempt from the challenges this life presents, but giving God the opportunity to awaken latent potential inside us redeems the pain.

Often, crises serve as painful catalysts that launch us forward if we allow them to do so. But of course, if we choose, we can sit down in our pain and let the circumstances overtake us. If we allow that to happen it will bring death to the potential that lies dormant inside us.

If we instead choose in the midst of our pain to set our eyes on our only *Answer*, we will be infused with faith that brings to us certain victory. We are changed through the process of learning to trust our *Source of hope*. And personal transformations take place when we accept our callings in faith.

We repeatedly see such transformations throughout both the Old and New Testaments. Abram became *Abraham*.[28] Although his wife was well beyond child-bearing age, and he had no children, God declared him *"the father of many nations."*

---

28 Genesis 17:5.

Sarai became *Sarah*. She would no longer be the barren, Sarai; she was to become Sarah, *"the mother of many nations,"* with kings of nations being among her descendants.[29]

Jacob became *Israel*—with God declaring that Jacob had *"struggled with God and with men and [had] prevailed."*[30] And Simon became *Peter*—the rock. Their new names served to be symbolic of how God changed their lives.

He is still changing lives today. God is the same yesterday, today, and forever,[31] and He is still *renaming* His children as he calls forth His intended purpose for our lives. So now, two more questions beg to be asked: First, what is God calling forth from your life? And second, will you accept and respond to His call with faith?

---

29 Genesis 17:15-16.
30 Genesis 32:28 (NKJV).
31 Hebrews 13:8.

CHAPTER 2

Beautifully Transformed

I LOVE HOW God keeps surprising me! Even as I encourage others to allow God to call them to action, He calls forth more and more from my own life, and I'm discovering new things about how God made me. And instead of just letting other people get to know the *real me* through my ministry, I feel like I'm finally getting to know myself! I feel like I am becoming more and more aware of how God has been transforming my life over time.

Uncovering God's plan for my life has become a great adventure as He keeps shining His light on the untapped gifts He has deposited in me. I'm finding that it's as if they have been placed in a secure vault for safekeeping until the right moment to unleash their potential. But even after the gifts have come to light I've had to learn by experience that the gifts God has placed in our lives aren't of best use until we give Him complete control of them.

The moment I chose to stop claiming the domain of my own life and allowed God full access, He stepped in to show me what He had in mind when He created me and placed gifts within me to be used for His glory and purpose.

That defining moment—when I realized yielding to my Creator was truly my only real option if I were to reach my potential—has served as the catalyst for what I call my permanent *life change*. I have realized a real transformation that only God could bring to me. He changed my perspective, and I no longer live to pursue my own dreams and desires. His dreams for my life have become my own, and my passionate pursuit of Him is now my heart's greatest desire.

Peter also experienced the type of transformation I'm talking about, and he echoed to others the calling he himself experienced in order to encourage them to accept the call of God for their own lives—to accept their calling to be transformed. Using the statement in Proverbs 3:34 as his text, here is what Peter said in his letter to the scattered Christians:

"God opposes the proud, but gives grace to the humble." [32]

---

32 "The LORD mocks the mockers but is gracious to the humble" (Proverbs 3:34).

*So humble yourselves under the mighty power of God, and
at the right time he will lift you up in honor.*

(1 Peter 5:5b-6)

Peter knew that it was his own pride, and his trust in his own strength, determination, and abilities, that became his downfall when he failed Jesus. He had to be humbled in order to receive from God what the Lord had to give to him. In spite of how strong Peter believed he and his faith were, he caved in under the pressure of the threat of personal harm. He denied Christ when his relationship with Jesus was challenged, and he must have hated himself for it.

Peter had experienced a closeness with Jesus that few of His disciples had known. He was among what many people call Jesus' *inner circle* of disciples. The inner circle is commonly seen to have been Simon Peter, John, and James the brother of John. Some theologians and commentators also include a fourth disciple in the inner circle—Andrew, the brother of Peter.

Jesus' closest disciples had walked with Him for three years. Over that time, Peter had come to lean on the strong but humble leadership of Jesus. When Jesus told His disciples He was leaving, it must have been difficult for Peter to imagine his life without Him, but he was determined never to abandon Jesus.

During their Passover meal—what we call the Last Supper—Jesus told His disciples He would be with them only a short while longer. And He told them where He was going, they couldn't come. This is how John later told the story:

> As soon as Judas left the room, Jesus said, "The time has come for the Son of Man to enter into his glory, and God will be glorified because of him. And since God receives glory because of the Son, he will give glory to the Son, and he will do so at once. Dear children, I will be with you only a little longer. And as I told the Jewish leaders, you will search for me, but you can't come where I am going."
>
> Simon Peter asked, "Lord, where are you going?"
>
> And Jesus replied, "You can't go with me now, but you will follow me later."
>
> "But why can't I come now, Lord?" he asked. "I'm ready to die for you."
>
> Jesus answered, "Die for me? I tell you the truth, Peter—before the rooster crows tomorrow morning, you will deny three times that you even know me."
>
> (John 13:31-33, 36-38)

Peter must have been confused by Jesus' words, but Jesus knew more about what was in Peter's heart than Peter himself did. Peter indeed ended up denying Christ, and all four of the Gospels record Peter's series of three indicting denials.

The passage in Mark ends with Jesus' piercing words echoing through Peter's mind, and Mark records that Peter *"broke down and wept."* [33]

But Luke's narrative about that incident is even more powerful and filled with emotion:

> *About an hour later someone else insisted, "This must be one of them, because he is a Galilean, too."*
>
> *But Peter said, "Man, I don't know what you are talking about." And immediately, while he was still speaking, the rooster crowed.*
>
> **At that moment the Lord turned and looked at Peter.** *Suddenly, the Lord's words flashed through Peter's mind: "Before the rooster crows tomorrow morning, you will deny three times that you even know me." And Peter left the courtyard, weeping bitterly.*
>
> (Luke 22:59-62) [emphasis mine]

I can't imagine Peter's pain at that moment as he looked into the eyes of Jesus. Peter knew he had failed. Imagine the remorse Peter must have felt! And then after Jesus was crucified, all of Peter's ability and hope to restore his broken relationship with his Lord must have seemed lost to him.

33 Mark 14:72.

This man, the Messiah—whom Peter had respected, revered, and loved—was gone, and Peter was left with only the guilt of irreconcilable regret. But of course we know that all was not lost for Peter. Even though he must have spent the time between the courtyard experience and the Resurrection in great remorse and pain, hope returned to him after Christ emerged from the tomb.

According to Mark's narrative, Mary Magdalene, Salome, and Mary the mother of James went to the tomb at sunrise on Sunday morning. When they arrived they saw the stone had been rolled away. When they looked into the tomb they could see that the body of Jesus was not there. Instead they saw an angel sitting on the right side of where the body had lain.

The women were startled, but the angel said to them:

Don't be alarmed. You are looking for Jesus of Nazareth, who was crucified. He isn't here! He is risen from the dead! Look, this is where they laid his body. Now go and tell his disciples, including Peter, that Jesus is going ahead of you to Galilee. You will see him there, just as he told you before he died. (Mark 16:6-7)

Peter was the only disciple the angel called out by name. After the women told Peter what the angel said, imagine how his hopes came gloriously alive to the possibility of once again seeing the look of love and acceptance on Jesus' face toward him! It's so beautiful that Jesus made such a special effort to let Peter know that He was specifically seeking him out following His resurrection. He wanted to be with *Peter*!

Peter knew what it was like to be absolutely crushed by the disappointment of his own sin and failure. Surely nothing could have been more important to him at that time than to experience restoration—to once again enjoy his relationship with Christ.

Peter had a problem, though, and he must have realized that the *person he was* didn't agree with who he wanted to be. But after hearing that the angel specifically mentioned him, Peter surely knew that the angel was pointing him to Jesus for the solution to his problem. For Peter, the angel's words were words of redemption. And Christ's clear plan for Peter's restoration not only proved to be enormously impactful in the early formation of the Church of Jesus Christ, the story behind it is also still powerfully illustrative today of God's willingness to forgive.

It should take no imagination on our part to think that Peter wanted to change. If he had not wanted to change he would have hidden from the resurrected Christ instead of humbly submitting to Him. His embarrassment over his failure could have kept him apart from Jesus if Peter had practiced avoidance of reality.

To receive the power to be changed, Peter had to choose to make himself available to the very one he had dishonored—the only *One* who could bring about the change he needed.

Making ourselves available to God's transformative power in our lives starts with our willingness to change. And our change is birthed in our ability to humbly recognize our need—to be truthfully self-aware. For Peter, he must have become painfully self-aware as the indicting words of denial he spoke moved across his lips. And his first action that eventually led him to being personally transformed had to have been his acknowledgment of failure and the sorrow he showed over his actions. Peter wept bitterly.

The sooner we admit our problems, the better it will go for us. If we don't acknowledge our failures quickly, we can fall into a pattern of trying to ignore and cover up our actions. We can attempt to neatly package our mistakes and keep them hidden away in our hearts. But if we don't deal with them, sooner or later those packages will become unraveled even as we cling to our attempts to protect ourselves from pain and guilt.

Being so confident and proud of our own abilities and strength that we cannot admit our failures will keep us from allowing our hearts to be exposed to the very possibility of change. Our lives will never be transformed into things of beauty unless we acknowledge our failures, accept our pain, and own our guilt.

Stuffing away and ignoring our embarrassment over possessing selfish views and motives only perpetuates a cancerous cycle of failure and disappointment. But admitting and facing our self-serving hearts, and opening them up to God, finally positions us for healing change.

Willingly admitting that we need an overhaul at the deepest level of our being launches us into an untapped, powerful realm. This is a key to surrender: admitting our absolute inadequacy in the presence of a completely sufficient God.

We can fail to realize how we limit ourselves by our unwillingness to surrender and submit ourselves to God. What we feel we can accomplish on our own may seem realistic, and we can think we're better off maintaining our hearts and emotions safely within our own control. But what God has to offer to people who willingly yield control of their lives to Him unleashes potential that can be gained no other way.

I am utterly amazed that we attempt to steadfastly hold on to what we perceive as control over our own lives. What we're really doing is holding on to a self-imposed ceiling that severely limits our God-given potential. We must learn to trade what's in *our* hand for what God holds in *His*. And that exchange requires complete trust. Peter chose to make that exchange.

We see strong evidence of Peter's surrender and reconciliation with Christ in chapter twenty-one of John's gospel account. I'm so glad the apostle John recorded the scene.

After the resurrection of Jesus, Peter and some of the other disciples decided to go on an all-night fishing expedition. Unfortunately, they caught nothing. As the morning light peeked over the horizon, the disappointed disciples saw the figure of a man standing on the beach.

They didn't realize the man was Jesus.

He called out, "Fellows, have you caught any fish?"

"No," they replied.

Then he said, "Throw out your net on the right-hand side of the boat, and you'll get some!"

So they did, and they couldn't haul in the net because there were so many fish in it. (John 21:5-6).

John recognized the imprint of the miraculous One upon what transpired there, and he shouted, *"It's the Lord!"* (v.7).

After Peter heard that, he wasted no time going overboard and swimming toward the Savior he so intensely loved—and needed. As they all enjoyed a breakfast of fish on the beach, the feeling of a healed relationship must have enveloped Peter.

Once his relationship with Christ was restored, Peter was ready to become the person God intended him to be. After Jesus ascended to Heaven, Peter obeyed Jesus and tarried with the other disciples in Jerusalem for the promised gift of the Holy Spirit. Ten days after the ascension, the Holy Spirit was poured out on all the believers who had gathered together there to pray.

As the Holy Spirit fell upon them, the believers began speaking in other languages—languages they had not learned. Crowds gathered around them in utter amazement. Fully forgiven and filled with the power of the Spirit of God, Peter then stepped forward to address the growing crowd.

With clarity, Peter explained Christ's crucifixion, His resurrection, His ascension, and the power of the Holy Spirit they were witnessing that day. He gave the people the opportunity to realize their sin in crucifying the Messiah; and Peter's words brought great conviction upon them.

Peter's words pierced their hearts, and they said to him and to the other apostles, "Brothers, what should we do?"

Peter replied, "Each of you must turn from your sins and turn to God, and be baptized in the name of Jesus Christ for the forgiveness of your sins. Then you will receive the gift of the Holy Spirit."   (Acts 2:37-38)

Peter found it! He found the ability to look past his own interests and focus on the interests of others. He found a new kind of boldness—one not based on self-confidence. He would never again be bothered by any fear to proclaim his association with Jesus. And Peter's newfound concern for others and their relationships with the living Christ became a foundation upon which the rest of his life was built.

The Bible tells us that Peter continued preaching to the people that day *"for a long time"* as he encouraged them to save themselves from the *"crooked generation"* they lived among. And after Peter pointed the people toward repentance, we are told that about 3,000 of them believed his message, were baptized, and were added to the Church that Jesus established that day.[34]

As those new believers—many of whom had traveled long distances in order to attend the feast in Jerusalem—returned to their homes, they took with them the gospel of Jesus Christ. The fire of Pentecost spread, and the world has never been the same. Peter traded his limited life of failure and self-protection for the Spirit-empowered life of a bold witness of Jesus Christ. That was the beginning of something miraculous!

Through the bold witness of the disciples of Jesus, the church at Jerusalem grew daily.[35] The believers learned to live together in love and unity as they worked through growing pains, disagreements, and opposition. The new

---

34 Acts 2:40-41.
35 Acts 2:47.

believers matured, and in the midst of growing persecution, they took the life-giving message of Jesus Christ outside of Jerusalem and Judea.

As Peter traveled and preached, people were healed. Then in one of the many cities he visited, he received a vision from God, in which Peter was instructed to share the good news of the salvation of Jesus Christ with the Gentiles.[36]

Three decades passed. By that time the New Testament Church had been successfully birthed and spread around the Roman empire, and fierce persecution had begun when Peter wrote his first epistle.

Peter knew what it was like to deny Christ, to be fully restored, and to be used to play an important role in beginning the greatest transformative movement the world has ever known. Peter's words certainly take on greater significance in light of his journey.

> *So humble yourselves under the mighty power of God, and*
> *at the right time he will lift you up in honor.*
>
> (1 Peter 5:6)

As we recognize Peter's beautifully transformed life, and as we follow the process of that transformation revealed in Scripture, we are inspired to examine ourselves. And we do well to ask ourselves why we are tempted to maintain,

---

36 Acts chapter 10.

defend, and protect our self-serving lives when God has so much more in mind for us.

God wants to transform all of us. But we'll never know what kind of change is possible in our lives until we're willing to open our hand that holds on to our pain and failures, let them go, and receive the beautiful transformation that God has in store for us!

CHAPTER 3

Perfectly Fitted Together

AS WE OPEN our hands to participate with God in what I'm calling the great exchange, we begin living in the freedom God intends for us. And as we read the Word of God and spend focused time with Him, the transformation begun in us continues to progress. Peter's transformation powerfully illustrates God's power to transform us; and clearly, the transformation that needs to take place in us includes a transformation of our minds.

God changed the way Peter thought, and He wants to change the way we think, too. The apostle Paul knew this, and here are words he shared with the church in Rome:

Don't copy the behavior and customs of this world, but let God transform you into a new person by changing the way you think. Then you will learn to know God's will for you, which is good and pleasing and perfect.

(Romans 12:2)

Paul told the believers in Rome that they needed to let God change the way they thought, and doing so would allow God to transform each of them into a new person. As we are transformed like that, our personal perspectives shift. We move beyond seeing things from limited, earthbound perspectives toward seeing things more through God's eyes. And seeing things from God's perspective gives us a clearer picture of His desires for our lives.

Our ability to *picture* ourselves fulfilling God's plans for our lives creates within us a burgeoning confidence. And that confidence allows us to take the first few adventurous steps in partnership with Him. Mental pictures can be powerful motivators. They can serve as encouragement to us for accomplishing our goals.

I was a gymnast in my middle-school and high-school years. In addition to much physical practice that was required of me, my coach instructed me to exercise my mind by picturing myself completing my routines with flawless accuracy. My coach told me to mentally repeat perfectly executed routines, not once, not twice, but many times. And I did as I was instructed. One specific gymnastics competition stands out in my memory because of the results of those mental exercises.

From about thirty minutes before my name was called to begin my balance beam routine, I sat, eyes closed, imagining myself executing each move flawlessly. I mentally executed tumbling passes and dance moves back and forth across the beam. And I imagined the mount and dismount at least a dozen times.

Each of my competitors that day had fallen off the balance beam at least once during their routines, and I knew their mistakes made it somewhat easier for me to win the balance beam competition. All I had to do was complete my routine without falling off, and I would have the honor of standing in first place during the awards ceremony.

As I mounted the balance beam, my muscles responded to my mental preparation. I performed each movement without losing my balance. I completed my routine and dismounted without major error. All my preparation, both physical and mental, paid off that day, and I won first place! Imagining myself walking through the paces of my goal had formed a mental pathway for a victorious reality.

Apparently, God designed us as humans to respond to both mental images (imagined scenes or events) and physical images (real, or historical events used for illustrations). Some examples in Scripture when God used imagery to relay His purposes readily come to mind. One of those times is when God used a physical image of the stars to create a mental picture for Abram to confirm His promise to him.

> Then the LORD took Abram outside and said to him, "Look up into the sky and count the stars if you can. That's how many descendants you will have!" And Abram believed the LORD, and the LORD counted him as righteous because of his faith. (Genesis 15:5-6)

And God gave the prophet Amos a vision one day. In the vision—a mental image—God used a plumb line to illustrate to Amos God's awareness of the sins of the citizens of the northern tribes of Israel, over whom King Jeroboam ruled.

> Then he showed me another vision. I saw the LORD standing beside a wall that had been built using a plumb line. He was using a plumb line to see if it was still straight. And the LORD said to me, "Amos, what do you see?"
>
> I answered, "A plumb line."
>
> And the LORD replied, "I will test my people with this plumb line. I will no longer ignore all their sins. The pagan

shrines of your ancestors will be ruined, and the temples of Israel will be destroyed; I will bring the dynasty of King Jeroboam to a sudden end." (Amos 7:7-9)

Then, God gave the prophet Jeremiah an illustrated message through the sight of a potter working at his wheel. In that message the Lord showed that He had the power and ability to remake the nation of Israel.

The LORD gave another message to Jeremiah. He said, "Go down to the potter's shop, and I will speak to you there." So I did as he told me and found the potter working at his wheel. But the jar he was making did not turn out as he had hoped, so he crushed it into a lump of clay again and started over.

Then the LORD gave me this message: "O Israel, can I not do to you as this potter has done to his clay? As the clay is in the potter's hand, so are you in my hand."

(Jeremiah 18:1-6)

With visual clarity, imagery can speak to us in ways mere words can't. And the apostle Peter seemed to inherently know this, or at least the Holy Spirit inspired him to use effective imagery when writing about the building of the Church. Referring back to the previously quoted passage from the second chapter of First Peter, notice that Peter portrayed the Church of Jesus Christ as a living, spiritual temple, with Christ as the cornerstone.

The Temple in Jerusalem was a beautiful edifice, and Peter used visual pictures of that temple to illustrate the idea of God constructing His Church as the spiritual temple that is the Body of Christ. He wrote:

> *You are coming to Christ, who is the living cornerstone of God's temple . . . And you are living stones that God is building into his spiritual temple.*   (1 Peter 2:4-5a)

Peter's analogy is beautifully appropriate. And as I studied Peter's words the Lord seemed to make it clear to me that it is when we are brought and fitted *together* that we are truly the living stones that make up God's Temple. And picture this: if we as the Body of Christ consistently applied this truth to the functioning of our individual and corporate lives, we would see a magnificence reminiscent of Solomon's Temple.

But unfortunately it is the tendency of many people to see themselves as simply individuals, standing alone, rather than important members of a larger community. And since we as Christians logically set a high priority on maintaining the health of our own personal relationships with God, we can easily become focused on our own needs and lose focus on the importance of applying ourselves to maintaining the welfare of the larger community of which we are a part. And in doing so, we can become guilty of ignoring the power and importance of Peter's Temple analogy.

In the building of Solomon's Temple, each stone used in the construction was carefully carved and fitted to the next—taking its place among the others to construct its breathtaking structure. We as individual believers are likewise being shaped to take our places alongside others in the walls of God's *spiritual temple.*

Just as the stones were fitted together to form the temple, all Christians are to be living stones fitted together to form one body of believers—one body, one spiritual temple, one Church of Jesus Christ. And together, as one body of believers who are carefully and perfectly fitted together, we are to represent God before mankind as the universal symbol of worship, devotion, and holy service.

According to the narrative in the book of First Kings, Solomon had a workforce of 80,000 workers who worked in the stone quarries to excavate and prepare the stone blocks for both the foundation and walls of the temple in Jerusalem.[37] And *"at the king's command, they quarried large blocks of high-quality stone and shaped them to make the foundation of the Temple"* (1 Kings 5:17).

Once the foundation was laid it was time to build the walls. And as we continue reading about the temple construction in First Kings, we read that there were no sounds of hammers or other tools required to quarry and shape the stones on the site of the building's construction.

---

37 1 Kings 5:15.

The stones used in the construction of the Temple were finished at the quarry, so there was no sound of hammer, ax, or any other iron tool at the building site.

(1 Kings 6:7)

Each stone was carefully sized, squared, and prepared in the quarry for its individual position in the Temple structure. It took careful planning and a great deal of work by many skilled craftsmen to prepare each individual stone before it was marked for its intended location in the structure and sent to the construction site.

Just as the stones were carefully prepared for use in the construction of the Jerusalem temple, we too have been prepared for our places in the structure of the Church of Jesus Christ. In fact, the planning and shaping of the living stones that we become began when we were formed in our mothers' wombs. Before anyone else could play a part in shaping us for use in God's Kingdom, God himself began forming us with extreme care. The psalmist David spoke of it this way:

You made all the delicate, inner parts of my body and knit me together in my mother's womb. Thank you for making me so wonderfully complex! Your workmanship is marvelous—and how well I know it.

(Psalm 139:13-14)

Because of the mark of the Master's hand on our lives, we are truly beautiful as individuals. But a different kind of beauty emerges as we allow our individuality to be positioned in the context of the larger Body of Christ—to become one part of a much larger and complete structure.

Our individual gifts and talents contribute to our uniqueness, but we weren't gifted to stand apart from our brothers and sisters in Christ; we were gifted to strengthen the whole Body. Verse seven of First Corinthians chapter twelve reminds us that *"a spiritual gift is given to each of us so we can help each other."* As we clothe ourselves with humility and immerse ourselves in the Christian community, the gifts and talents God has given us are empowered for their intended purpose in our lives.

The Bible reminds us that we're better together:

Two people are better off than one, for they can help each other succeed. If one person falls, the other can reach out and help. But someone who falls alone is in real trouble. Likewise, two people lying close together can keep each other warm. But how can one be warm alone? A person standing alone can be attacked and defeated, but two can stand back-to-back and conquer. Three are even better, for a triple-braided cord is not easily broken.

(Ecclesiastes 4:9-12)

Our giftings and talents can eventually become unused and diminished when we isolate ourselves, because they are intended to reflect God's glory *through* our lives to others. But when we stand alongside others and use our gifts and talents within the corporate Body of Christ, God blesses them and causes them to flourish and grow. Through them we are capable of significantly impacting entire generations. And in fact, that is exactly what God wants to do through us.

The Bible contains many stories about how people were enabled and used by God to affect not only those who lived during their own times but also future generations. Peter was of course one of those people, but another person comes to mind as I contemplate how our involvement in God's plan affects others. I am thinking about David, the one God called a *"man after my own heart."* [38]

David was gifted and skilled in many areas; he is known as being a shepherd, musician, poet, soldier, prophet, and king. As David pursued God's heart in all those callings, his gifts and talents remained submitted to God's purposes in his life.

In our zeal to use our gifts, people can fall prey to an all-too-human tendency to pursue their gifts instead of the God

---

38 Acts 13:22; 1 Samuel 13:14.

who gave them. But we do not read in the Bible about David making that mistake. Even though David had moments of failure in his life, we know that he was always determined to use whatever abilities he had been given to fulfill God's plan for using his life to benefit God's kingdom.

As a man of faith, David was a true man of God. He was called and appointed by God. He was gifted, talented, and enabled by God to lead. As king he expanded the kingdom and gained great wealth and influence. But even as king of the united kingdom of Israel, David didn't always get his way as an individual follower of God. David desired to build a magnificent Temple for God, but God wouldn't let him do it.

Instead of allowing David to build a permanent temple in Jerusalem to replace the wilderness tabernacle, God determined to have the temple built by David's son, Solomon. David knew of God's intentions for a long time— even before Solomon was born. Many years later, David sent for Solomon and gave him these instructions:

> *"My son, I wanted to build a Temple to honor the name of the LORD my God," David told him. "But the LORD said to me, 'You have killed many men in the battles you have fought. And since you have shed so much blood in my sight, you will not be the one to build a Temple to honor my name. But you will have a son who will be a man of*

peace. I will give him peace with his enemies in all the surrounding lands. His name will be Solomon, and I will give peace and quiet to Israel during his reign. He is the one who will build a Temple to honor my name. He will be my son, and I will be his father. And I will secure the throne of his kingdom over Israel forever.'"

(1 Chronicles 22:7-10)[39]

David eagerly wanted to build a house for the Lord, and he had the abilities and access to the resources to allow him to construct it. David could have used his abilities, wealth, and influence to disobey God and start building the temple. But instead of focusing on himself and his own desires and gifts, he focused on fulfilling the plan God determined for the future. David spent the last years of his life equipping Solomon for his future task and amassing many of the materials his son used to build the temple.[40]

It had to have been a humbling experience to be so gifted, so talented, so able, so visionary, so desirous of success, and so experienced, and yet be satisfied with preparing someone else to do what David's heart drove him to accomplish. But we can find ourselves in similarly humbling positions while serving God's Kingdom as we are called upon to support the work and future of others in the Church.

---

39 See also 2 Samuel 7:1-17 and 1 Chronicles 17:1-15.
40 1 Chronicles 22:5.

In fact, just as David had to start focusing on the future and work of his son, we can also come to the place of needing to prioritize the work of our own children to accomplish much in the future that we will not be able to accomplish during our lives.

As my children have grown into adulthood and left home, I have been faced with the reality of being in what I would call the *middle* generation. And that has caused me to feel increasing responsibility for mentoring the next generation.

I understand that I must become a bridge over which God can travel to equip members of the next generation to fulfill their destinies. I know I must lead by empowering others. No longer are my own visions of grandeur in leadership and great personal accomplishments appropriate. (I say this with just a little *tongue in cheek* since such self-focused things were never really appropriate—just sort of youthful arrogance.)

In recent years I have actually found an amazing sense of fulfillment in the work of empowering others. And this sense of fulfillment isn't limited to just empowering the next generation. What I call our *Kingdom Influence* can project to each generation—to those walking ahead of us, those running beside us, and those coming behind us.

And today, as I joyfully sow into the lives of others, no matter their seasons in life, I encourage them to live as part of the whole—the collective Body of Christ. God designed us to be both fully dependent on Him and interdependent within His Body. We truly need each other, and not just because we may feel incomplete without one another, but because as individual stones in God's spiritual temple, we simply cannot fulfill our corporate calling alone.

Peter knew that each of us is just one, single, living stone used by God to build the Church of Jesus Christ. And as we read what Peter had to say, it becomes clear that as long as people are being called to salvation and service in the Kingdom, God will continue to build the Church—with one living stone fit alongside the others, and all built upon Christ, the Cornerstone.

Peter knew in his day that the Church was yet to be completed. And still today God means for the Church to grow and become not only larger but more beautiful over time. Peter encouraged his readers to understand that each of them was a living stone, and it took all the living stones to build the Church. Each individual stone is important, but it is when all the stones are placed together that the Church grows toward completion. With that picture in mind, here are some questions for you:

Are you willing to submit your own individuality to the larger interests of the Kingdom? Will you recognize and value yourself as one of the living stones God is using to build the Church—the spiritual temple that will never pass away?

Following His resurrection, Jesus spoke these words before His ascension to heaven:

Therefore, go and make disciples of all the nations, baptizing them in the name of the Father and the Son and the Holy Spirit.   (Matthew 28:19)

We call this charge the *Great Commission*. And it remains the mandate of the Church today. Jesus is still calling us to take our eyes off ourselves, put them on the world of people yet untouched by His love, and show willingness to reach them at any cost. This kind of selfless focus requires us to submit our individual gifts and interests to the good of the Kingdom of God through the Church, the *Body of Christ*.

While we might like to stop and build for ourselves a fulfilling, comfortable life, He is urging us to keep moving and make the spiritual welfare of others our focus. But this is counterintuitive to our selfish natures, so we need extra help to overcome temptations to focus merely on our own personal interests. I am not alone in my belief that our greatest help in correcting our perspectives is reading the Bible, God's Holy Word. We should read it continually.

We limit the potential of our Kingdom influence in the lives of others as we allow ourselves to be distracted by the world around us that encourages us to selfishly focus on our own lives and our own plans. But the Word counteracts in so many ways the culture in which we find ourselves physically and, too often, emotionally immersed. As we focus outward with a godly perspective on life and service, the ceiling over our influence lifts, and we become exponentially more useful to the Kingdom of God.

My prayer for you is that your heart will be drawn to God's heart for all people as you saturate your life with His words. May His adventurous plans for your life become more desirable to you than the limiting thoughts of a comfortable existence. And may your focus become set on being one living stone perfectly fitted together with others in the Church—God's spiritual temple that exists on Earth today—as we become better equipped to carry out the work of His Kingdom in this generation and those to come.

CHAPTER 4

Leading by Example

I HAVE BEEN reminded over the years that it is important for people to lead by example, and I've learned through many experiences that is true. But I don't suppose I've ever been more aware than now just how crucial it is that I live my life in such a way that others can follow—that I am leading by living the life I am encouraging them to live. It is important that leaders lead, not push, other people toward the goals they pursue.

As I consider this, I understand that, as a leader, Peter could not always point to his past decisions and his past actions as examples to show others how they should behave—to prove to them they could have confidence in his leadership. But Peter could certainly use his past failures to show how he had changed to become an effective, powerful, but humble leader. And he could do that because he learned from his mistakes and indeed became a leader worth emulating.

Hopefully, you and I are also becoming the leaders God wants us to be in spite of our own past weaknesses and failures. Clearly, for all of us, the success of our progress in maturing into leaders worth following depends largely on the way we have dealt with personal issues of disobedience and our abilities to not only hear God's voice but to faithfully follow it.

Most of us have adventurous stories from our childhood that make us shake our heads and laugh as we remember them. Whether it was jumping off roofs or playing chicken, as we consider decisions we made in the past we are sometimes amazed that we made it to adulthood without significant injury—or made it here at all!

My mother has reminded me numerous times of a certain joyride I took as a five-year old little girl—no, not in a car; my bicycle (recently freed from its training wheels at the time) was my preferred mode of transportation.

We lived near the bottom of a steep hill in a lovely neighborhood. I think Mom could sense my longing to ride the hill, to feel the wind in my face as I descended down the hill. And her stern words to me conveyed her growing suspicion.

"Debbie, if you ride down that hill, we will punish you."

To most children, the threat of being punished would suffice as an effective deterrent. However, I guess I wasn't like most children. I walked away from her firm warning and weighed the situation in my young mind as if I were making a logical business decision. And that hill was awfully enticing!

I made my decision without much hesitation; I decided the thrill was indeed worth whatever consequence I would experience. After all, punishment was only momentary pain, but I was sure I would remember forever the thrill of riding down the hill. Going outside to play one afternoon, I decided that was my moment—my long-awaited opportunity.

Up the hill I trudged, pushing my bike until I reached the highest point on the hill to begin my descent. Of course, like all conscientious riders, I looked both ways before heading to the middle of the street. I mounted my bike and peddled for all I was worth to gain maximum speed. And within seconds I lifted my feet to enjoy the ride of my life.

Apparently Mom and Dad walked out of the front door just in time to see my blonde ponytail sail by. Just past our house was a cross street that was heavily traveled, and I was heading for the crossing. With no ability to stop the potentially horrific situation they were watching, I imagine my parents' prayer lives rose to a new level.

Much to their relief, I coasted to a stop just short of the cross street. I walked my bike back to the house and presented myself to Mom and Dad. I awaited my punishment feeling the ride was totally worth whatever retribution I was about to receive. And, yes, my parents followed through on their word.

My young mind weighed the options and made a decision to ignore the danger and the prospect of punishment for blatantly disobeying my mother. I chose to endure the punishment so I could enjoy the pleasure of the moment. Today we laugh about the foolish decision I made as a five-year-old. But that's only because the five-year-old lived through the experience.

The outcome of my bicycle thrill ride could have turned out very differently. All it would have taken to change my life forever (or end it) was one driver of a car not seeing me and pulling out in front of me—or for me to have not stopped before coming to the cross street. Mom knew that, hence her warning to me.

As their children, our parents warn us of danger, and we decide whether or not we are going to heed their warnings. As God's children, *He* issues warnings to us, too; and regardless of our age when we receive them, we also decide how to respond to *His* directions. We certainly need to make wise decisions when choosing whether or not we heed God's instructions. Obeying God is wisdom well applied.

We place ourselves in potentially precarious situations when we unwisely make choices based on our own desires rather than being motivated by obedience and godly wisdom. We have a much better chance of making sound decisions as we learn to fill ourselves with God's Word and walk obediently in step with the Spirit of God.

Parents have experience and the ability to anticipate danger, but God's understanding is absolutely unlimited. He sees the end from the very beginning, and He often sends the most dependable warnings in our direction to keep us out of trouble.

If we learn to stay in tune with God, we will more readily pick up on even His most gentle nudging. But even though we may have become tender toward His gently-provided directions, we must still decide if we are either going to receive them and obey them in humility, or decide to ignore them and go our own way.

When I look at Simon Peter's life, I perceive some similarities between his approach to life and mine as I was growing up. Being forthright, persistent, and a bit sassy certainly described me, and the same qualities probably could also have been used to describe Peter. But I meant well as a young person, and I believe Peter always meant well, too.

But like *my* actions sometimes, even though Peter's motivation may have seemed rightly placed, his execution was sometimes way off. One time that happened was when Peter used his sword to slash off the right ear of the high priest's servant, Malchus.[41]

Peter did that before Jesus' crucifixion, when the Roman soldiers and Temple guards came to the Garden of Gethsemane at night to arrest Jesus. Peter acted with good intentions in an attempt to protect Jesus, but that is not how Jesus wanted Peter to respond. Jesus restored the man's ear and corrected Peter for his impetuous, passionate act.[42]

Just as we make mistakes, so did Peter; and as we discussed earlier, he even made the mistake of denying Christ. But once his old nature was broken and he was fully surrendered and yielded to the Holy Spirit, Peter's actions not only became vital to the birth of the Church, but his life and ministry also were used to affect Church history forever.

Founded upon the truth of Peter's confession of faith and established by the long-awaited Messiah, who became the *Cornerstone* for God's spiritual temple, the Church of Jesus Christ was built, and the world has simply never been the same.

Peter's letter to his scattered brothers and sisters in Christ unveils the strength of his maturity that was woven

---

41 John 18:10; Luke 22:47-50.
42 John 18:11; Luke 22: 51.

into his thirty years of ministry following Jesus' death and resurrection. In verse three of First Peter chapter five, Peter counseled those who were appointed as elders over God's flock and said to them, *"lead them by your own good example."*

Learning to walk, or live, in such a way that others will follow isn't always easy, but it's necessary. Peter knew that, and he was careful to remind others of its importance. Depending on where we start in our discipleship, this way of living—being a good example—can require a huge transformational shift in perspective. And changes to our perspectives often come at the hand of correction and difficult circumstances.

Correction brings us discomfort, and having to deal with difficult circumstances as a result of our bad decisions causes us frustration and pain. And these things have a way of getting our attention. Our daily routine is upended by them; and when that happens, if we are wise we begin searching for solutions to the problems they bring.

When we respond by searching for solutions to our problems in the right place, correction and difficulties can become the doors that grant us entrance into the wisdom and humility we need to be equipped for leadership. They lead us into a deeper surrender of our will to God. And as we surrender our will to Him, we come to a place where we can yield to him not only our frustration and pain but also all our unanswered questions and confusion.

With our questions and confusions turned over to the Lord, we learn humility, gain experience by depending on Him to lead us, and grow in strength through trusting Him to deal with all of life's issues. Only with humility, experience, and strength—such important tools for leadership—are we positioned to lead others on the path toward Christian maturity and increased faith.

Peter's comforting letter sent to the persecuted believers from his position of leadership served as an encouragement to them. When Peter spoke of the challenges of persecution, he knew what he was talking about. And by using the leadership skills he possessed, he could encourage them with understanding and confidence.

Peter knew persecution from first-hand experience. (And according to long-held tradition, his life was eventually ended by those who persecuted him.) But Peter didn't shrink back in fear during times of persecution. Rather, he led his brothers and sisters in Christ by example, and he reminded them of what persecution was doing for them:

> *These trials will show that your faith is genuine. It is being tested as fire tests and purifies gold—though your faith is far more precious than mere gold. So when your faith remains strong through many trials, it will bring you much praise and glory and honor on the day when Jesus Christ is revealed to the whole world.* (1 Peter 1:7)

And so it is with us. If allowed to do so, persecution will refine and strengthen us.

But *fiery trials* cause us to make choices. Will we turn our eyes toward Heaven with complete surrender in our hearts, present our trouble to God, allow Him to show us His solution, and trust Him for it? Or will we struggle to manufacture our own solution to our upended circumstance? The first choice will lead us toward living a life worth emulating and fit us for leadership; the other will lead us toward self-focused ineffectiveness.

To be effective leaders—to effectively represent Christ— we must keep our lives focused on fulfilling God's will and our mission, which is meeting the needs of others. But with so much promotion of self-interests all around us, and with the goal of avoiding discomfort so readily evident in our society, we occasionally need Peter and others to remind us of what's important.

My daughter, Kirsten, and I were doing a little shopping the other day, and as we walked through a busy shopping mall going from store to store I was suddenly struck once again by how futile so many of our pursuits can be. To be too caught up in day-to-day concerns that benefit us only from an earthly perspective, and to lose ourselves in making our lives as comfortable as possible, is to forget our greater purpose.

There's nothing wrong with enjoying the pleasures God affords us in this life, but if we're not careful we can easily become enamored with them and lose spiritual focus. Although our self-focused behavior may seem inconsequential in the moment, losing *Kingdom focus* will, in the long run, result in our loss of *Kingdom influence*.

While leading others to know and follow after Christ, the influence we gain in the Kingdom becomes the spiritual legacy that we share and leave to others—the legacy of a faithful heart toward God. To live our own lives faithfully before others is to prove our loyalty toward our Lord by knowing His Word and obediently choosing to do what it says. As we do that, we pass on to others the example of a life spiritually well-lived. As Christ's representatives, we must walk in God's ways in order to show others *the Way*.

There are two very sobering verses in the Old Testament book of Jeremiah that come to mind as I think on this. They state the consequences of following our own ways instead of walking in God's:

> *These wicked people refuse to listen to me. They stubbornly follow their own desires and worship other gods. Therefore, they will become like this loincloth—good for nothing! As a loincloth clings to a man's waist, so I created Judah and*

Israel to cling to me, says the LORD. They were to be my people, my pride, my glory—an honor to my name. But they would not listen to me. (Jeremiah 13:10-11)

We don't like to think of ourselves as wicked, but when we choose to be caught up in our own lives and pursuits, we separate ourselves from God's agenda and begin acting outside of the parameters He set for us. And by continuing to do that, we *"will become ... good for nothing!"* This is the result of the self-focused ineffectiveness that I mentioned earlier.

So, how do we produce a life worth emulating? We start by making reading His Word and aligning our lives with it our priority. With that in mind, the following passage from chapter two of First Peter becomes incredibly challenging.

For God is pleased when, conscious of his will, you patiently endure unjust treatment. Of course, you get no credit for being patient if you are beaten for doing wrong. But if you suffer for doing good and endure it patiently, God is pleased with you. For God called you to do good, even if it means suffering, just as Christ suffered for you. He is your example, and you must follow in his steps.

He never sinned, nor ever deceived anyone. He did not retaliate when he was insulted, nor threaten revenge when he suffered. He left his case in the hands of God, who always judges fairly. He personally carried our sins in his

body on the cross so that we can be dead to sin and live
for what is right. By his wounds you are healed. Once you
were like sheep who wandered away. But now you have
turned to your Shepherd, the Guardian of your souls.

(1 Peter 2:19-25)

Jesus Christ took our sins upon himself. He allowed himself to be crucified in our place. And He healed us from the disease of our souls. What mercy! What incredible grace we have received! Because He bore our sinfulness, we are freed from its grip, and we are free to *"live for what is right."*

One of the greatest sins we can commit is to not truly trust what the Lord says and, consequently, stray from His commands. In doing that, we stray from the watchful care of our *Shepherd.* He is the *Guardian of our souls.* His words spoken to us guide us and keep us from harm. They are of utmost importance, and yet many people treat Him as if His admonitions were simply a handful among a smorgasbord of choices that we can either accept or reject.

The children of Israel were condemned for having such views.

As for you, O people of Israel, this is what the Sovereign
LORD says: Go right ahead and worship your idols, but
sooner or later you will obey me and will stop bringing
shame on my holy name by worshiping idols.

(Ezekiel 20:39)

People sometimes act as if they have the option of keeping God as merely one among the many objects of their attention and devotion. But He will not allow himself to be placed among gods whom people serve to their own undoing. He loves us too much to leave us in such indecision and complacency. As Christian leaders we must not fall prey to such a misdirected mindset. If we do, we will lead people only to destruction.

We find true joy and our greatest freedom in positioning ourselves in a place of obedience under the hand of Christ. He truly is our *Shepherd*, and He provides for us a spiritual sheepfold where we can remain protected in His care. It is only our disobedience—our own decisions—that can lead us into a position that is outside of His protection. Without willingly remaining under His care and supervision, we open ourselves up to potential dangers and unnecessary evils.

Why, then, do leaders stray? Do they not appreciate His watchful care? Do they not take seriously the threat of the enemy of our souls? Like teenagers who seek to rebel against their parents' authority, leaders, too, can fall into attempting to free themselves from the very protective care they so desperately need. To keep this from happening to us—to remain leaders who lead by godly example—it is crucial for us to deliberately surrender our will to God and obey Him.

Just as children honor their parents by obeying them, if we truly accept our precious Lord for who He is, we will have no trouble honoring Him and placing ourselves in His loving and capable hands. If, on the other hand, we yield to our desires and allow our own wants and wishes to lead us and mandate our actions, we risk falling into discounting Christ's leadership and choosing to live however we deem fit. And dishonoring God with our lives will affect our ability to lead others to know and honor God with their lives.

In order for us to lead by example, we must first submit ourselves to God's care and authority—submit to His leadership. Then we can lead. We can lead by example in our families. We can lead by example as we work in our local churches. We can lead by example as we join other members of the Body of Christ in fulfilling the Great Commission. And we can lead by example in both the good times and bad, the happy times and sad, and even in times of persecution and suffering.

> For God called you to do good, even if it means suffering, just as Christ suffered for you. He is your example, and you must follow in his steps. (1 Peter 2:21)

Jesus led by example. Peter led by example. And we must lead by example. But ultimately, it is our choice to either lead by example—with the welfare of others in mind—or go our own way and prove ourselves to be unproductive and ill-equipped to lead.

I invite you to join me in doing everything we can to properly lead by example. Together we will join not only our voices but also our actions—our lives—to promote and bring glory to the Kingdom.

CHAPTER 5

Walking Forward Unafraid

THE GOOD EXAMPLE we provide to others through our confident, Christlike living shines brightly as we boldly tackle life's many trials and adventures. And our confidence in walking with the Lord grows as we continue to trust His leading and lean into His watchful care over our lives.

Our developing confidence often becomes apparent in our determination to overcome fear as we walk forward in life accompanied by Christ's comforting presence. I am determined to grow more confident in God and my calling; so over the last several years, I have deliberately chosen to put myself in situations where I've had to face fear head-on.

A productive way to grow in boldness is to work on conquering fear.

I always wanted to go skydiving. To courageously free fall with the wind in my face was an exhilarating thought (sounds a little like my bicycle thrill ride when I was five years old, doesn't it). My fiftieth birthday proved to be the perfect opportunity for me to fulfill my long-awaited dream of skydiving. Most people might not choose to jump out of a perfectly good airplane; but once again, I guess I'm not *most people.*

So I determined to celebrate my birthday by jumping out of a plane, and I went about making mental preparations for it. My most pressing prayer leading up to the jump was that I would not be afraid. I wanted to enjoy every minute of the experience without that proverbial sick feeling in the pit of the stomach that so often goes along with fear. I assumed I would probably attempt the free-fall adventure from 14,000 feet up in the air *only once,* so I didn't want to waste a moment worrying.

I've watched many people fearfully approach challenging life experiences, and I've sometimes seen their fears rob them of enjoying incredible opportunities. I knew I didn't want that to happen to me. People often shy away from living boldly when they become afraid. Even as Christians who stand on the firm foundation of an all-powerful God, we can too easily give in to fear. Fear tends to be a paralyzing agent, and it can keep us from taking that *next step*, from trying that *new thing*, or even from meeting that *unfamiliar person*.

However, I've watched other people approach challenging life experiences in a way that made it appear they had absolutely no apprehensions at all attempting to hold them back. That's how I wanted it to be with me. I wanted (and continue to want now) to look fear in the face and refuse to allow it to keep me from walking forward with confidence into my next experience—into my next appointment in life.

But we all experience fear on some level. And when watching how people handle fear, I've noticed that the same fear that paralyzes one person from taking an action is easily overcome by others. It seems to me that the difference maker for the ones who move beyond their fears in order to follow their dreams and callings is their determination to move forward despite the fear or trepidation they feel.

Like happiness, sadness, grief, and hurt, fear is a feeling—an emotion. The intensity of our emotional responses—or the degree to which we allow them to affect our actions—is lessened as we train ourselves to not be overly influenced by feelings.

For instance, when we're sad we can train ourselves to not dwell on our sadness to the point that it becomes debilitating. Properly handling our sadness will eventually yield to a more balanced emotional state. And likewise, when the importance we place on our own feeling of happiness threatens to lead us into becoming self-centered, we can train ourselves to maintain self-control and not exaggerate our own importance.

We experience emotional balance when we learn to balance our feelings.

When it comes to fear, I'm convinced that if we don't feed its intensity by worrying about the things we fear, it loses its grip on us. So teaching ourselves to *starve the fear* by choosing to not worry becomes a meaningful objective for us to purposely pursue if we intend to walk forward unafraid as we approach any challenge.

In my sky-diving adventure, I certainly had numerous opportunities to practice starving fear. The day of my big jump proved to be one exercise after another in overcoming the temptation to fear.

I was pleased that my oldest daughter and her husband chose to join me in my great adventure. My husband and I drove to the jump site, where they met us. The drive to the jump site seemed much longer than the two hours it took to get there.

I must admit, two hours to think about jumping from the safety of an airplane at 14,000 feet is a long time.

To complicate matters, it was raining as we were leaving the Nashville area. For a *safe novice* skydiving experience, the jump site needs to be free of cloud cover, and the winds must be mostly calm. Jumping in unstable weather can be dangerous, and the jump coaches and pilots will shut down the process if they feel the conditions are worsening.

An impending storm over middle Tennessee wasn't proving to be much of an encouragement to us, but we kept driving. As we drove, I asked the Lord to give us a window of clear skies and calm winds for the jump. After all, I'd waited a long time for that moment, and I didn't want to back down for any reason, including weather.

We arrived at the jump site to find a backlog of people waiting for the weather to cooperate. Then an administrative glitch in our processing caused yet one more delay. More waiting meant more time to stew. Our names were finally called, and we went through our mandatory training and outfitting—then, even more waiting.

But finally a weather window opened, and we were given the *all clear* to load the plane. "Thank you, Lord, for answering my adventurous prayer," I said as we prepared to depart.

We taxied, took off, reached the proper altitude, and circled around and waited as the pilot tried to decide whether it was safe to jump. By that point, I think my son-in-law was growing a little nervous!

The pilot shouted, "It's now or never!" and the door opened. My daughter's tandem-jump coach slid toward the door with my daughter in tow, and out they went. Her husband and his coach followed suit with no time to hesitate.

Then it was my turn. The last thing I remember my jump-coach shouting to me was, "Remember to breathe!"

Point taken! It turned out that breathing was actually not a problem, though. As I left the plane, instinct took over, and screaming ensued. Sort of like how spanking initiates the first cries of a baby, apparently sheer exhilaration (or terror?) must force people to breathe when they jump out of a plane!

I regained my composure about fifteen seconds into the jump, and I was absolutely mesmerized by the freedom of falling—and the incredible view. I felt as if the air were holding me up rather than feeling like my body was accelerating toward the ground. The world below me seemed like a still shot photo—a beautiful picture, frozen in time, taken from high above. I was enjoying the moment with no fear!

Much too soon in my opinion, my jump-coach pulled the cord. The parachute opened, and we navigated our way toward the target landing zone.

Wow! What an incredibly exhilarating experience that was!

And as it turned out, the only sick feeling I had in the pit of my stomach was from taking too many quick spinning turns with the parachute as my jump-coach let me have the reigns for a few moments.

Joy-riding seems to be a consistent theme in my life!

Just as we removed our gear, skydiving opportunities for

the remainder of the day were called off. There was no more jumping that day due to the weather.

I appreciate God's perfectly wrapped gifts of momentary, adventurous joy in my life. It seemed like every step along the way in my skydiving experience offered me an opportunity to give in to fear and opt out of the adventure. And I'm so glad I didn't take any of those fear-induced opportunities!

I personally chose a risk-taking adventure, and by doing that, I also willingly chose to deal with the feelings of fear and apprehension that decision brought to me. Many times, though, feelings of fear can come our way as a result of no decisions we make personally. But regardless of how feelings of fear and trepidation come to us, the importance of choosing to not worry about them remains the same—even in those moments when we are blindsided by unwelcome trials.

For example, when the pantry and the bank account are empty at the same time, we have a choice to make: Will we accommodate fear by worrying? Or will we look to God, who supplies all our needs?[43] Will we despair in fear or declare with Solomon, *"The Lord will not let the godly go hungry"*?[44]

And when the doctor's report has given us less than six months of life remaining, will we succumb to naturally-ensuing fear or choose to speak the words of the psalmist, *"I*

---

43 Philippians 4:19.
44 Proverbs 10:3a.

will not die; instead, I will live to tell what the Lord has done"?[45]

Further, when we suffer injustice, will we let fear drive us toward a closed heart, bitterness, and retaliation against someone who causes us to fear by threatening or mistreating us, or will we choose to respond like Christ? Peter addressed such suffering—and how Christ properly responded to it—in his letter to his brothers and sisters in Christ. He said of Jesus:

> *He did not retaliate when he was insulted, nor threaten revenge when he suffered. He left his case in the hands of God, who always judges fairly.*　　(1 Peter 2:23)

Jesus did not allow fear to motivate Him to take any action against those who threatened and persecuted Him. When He was threatened and persecuted, He simply left His situation in the hands of the Father. Peter also learned to do that, and his words remind us today that if we are to be like Christ, we must choose to face our fear with confidence in God's ability to orchestrate a just outcome in our situation.

From much of what we read in the Bible about Peter we may hesitate to want to believe he ever feared anything. He always seemed not only impulsive but also strong and fearless even to the point of endangering his own life. Witness his attack on Malchus, which we discussed earlier.

But of course there were times—two particular times—

---

45 Psalm 118:17.

when Peter's actions revealed that even *he* was susceptible to feeling fear. And in both instances his fear was linked to the possibility that he could lose his life.

The first was when the Lord invited Peter to walk to him on the water. In Matthew chapter fourteen we read that Jesus sent his disciples across the Sea of Galilee in a boat while he remained for a while on shore. During the night, before the sun rose in the morning,[46] the waves were heavy as the boat struggled against the wind.

Then the disciples looked across the waves and saw Jesus walking toward them on the water. They were frightened and thought Jesus was a ghost. Seeing someone walking on the water at night—perhaps highlighted by the moon or a slight peeking of the sun's light over the horizon before sunrise—was, indeed, probably a little disconcerting.

> *But Jesus spoke to them at once. "Don't be afraid," he said. "Take courage. I am here!"*
>
> *Then Peter called to him, "Lord, if it's really you, tell me to come to you, walking on the water."*
>
> *"Yes, come," Jesus said.* (Matthew 14:27-29)

Peter called out to Jesus in his impetuousness, and he stepped out of the boat onto the water in his boldness. Peter indeed walked on the water. But before reaching Jesus,

---

46 The Bible says this was during the night's "fourth watch"—understood to be between 3:00 AM and 6:00 AM according to many sources.

he took his eyes off of his destination and placed it on the surrounding wind and waves.

> *But when he saw the strong wind and the waves, he was terrified and began to sink. "Save me, Lord!" he shouted.*
>
> *Jesus immediately reached out and grabbed him. "You have so little faith," Jesus said. "Why did you doubt me?"*
>
> (Matthew 14:30-31)

Matthew said Peter was *terrified*. Peter experienced true fear that night.

The second time we know that Peter experienced fear was when he was challenged in the High Priest's courtyard as the Jewish officials were deciding what to do with Jesus after leading Him away in the dead of night from where He was praying in Garden of Gethsemane. All four of the gospel writers recorded the fear that motivated Peter to deny Christ.[47]

Jesus had been taken, and it was clear that His enemies were planning on having Him killed. Peter feared that his life, too, would be in jeopardy if he were to be revealed as a follower of Christ; and that was the motivation for Peter's denial.

But Peter learned the lessons his experiences with fear taught him, and he didn't let his fear stop him from following Jesus and becoming one of the principal leaders in

---

47 Matthew 26:69-75; Mark 14:66-71; Luke 22:54-63; John 18:15-27.

the Church during his lifetime. Peter showed determination to rise above both his failures and his fears. I believe Peter, too, learned to *starve* his fears. He learned to deny his own emotions and follow boldly after God and the ministry to which he was called.

Peter put his courtyard experience behind him and walked forward unafraid. And so must we. We must put behind us any *courtyard* experience or sinking terror we have felt and refuse to succumb to any fear that would hold us back from faithfully responding to and following our Lord.

Succumbing to fear can position us as victims, and viewing ourselves as victims can cause us to become consumed with our own self-interests. We can become self-centered and self-serving as we continue to dwell on our *victimhood*. However, choosing confidence in Christ and His Word can lift us from the status of a victim and position us as victors in faith. The choice to refuse to walk in fear and walk instead in faith is ours to make. And the choice to overcome fear with faith leads us into living an adventurous life with Christ.

As we walk closely with God, He enables us to more readily access His promises, and that grants us strength in Christ as one fear after another is dispelled. But know this: having the fortitude to live this way requires determination on our part. And it certainly requires us to focus on God and His purposes for us rather than on any circumstances that tend to produce fear in us.

As of this writing, I have watched my mom bravely battle the disease of cancer over the last three years. Although the prognosis given by the doctor today continues to be that the cancer is terminal, Mom has chosen to focus on the goodness of God instead of any fear she has of the disease. Some days, she is free of most of the side effects of the medication, and some days she's not. But throughout the surgeries, chemotherapy, immunotherapy, blood tests, side effects, and threat of imminent death, she has maintained gratitude toward God and a sense of true peace as she chooses to trust her Savior.

She knows I'm watching her navigate difficult circumstances, and she knows her grandchildren are watching her, too. Mom is making quite an impact on all of us as she models before us what trust in the goodness and the love of God looks like. I think she would rather be at home in Heaven with her Savior than continue to fight for life here on Earth, but she chooses to stay engaged in the battle until her time here is complete. Mom walks in close relationship with God and lets His Word guide her steps through the difficulties.

Choosing to actively maintain trust in God's goodness and love requires that we spend time pursuing God through

His Word and prayer. But even if taking the time to learn what God's Word has to say about our life situations seems to be too great a responsibility of time or effort for us, Mom's living example before us is inescapable.

This makes me ask, what are we teaching people by our words and actions? Are we projecting faith or fear? Are we walking forward unafraid or shrinking backward in fear?

What we focus on matters. Our choices matter. We reveal to others the hope and confidence we have in our lives by the choices we make.

As they are growing up, our children are certainly recipients of messages learned from our examples even if no one else notices (which of course is not possible). And I am keenly aware that my life still shapes my children's lives even into adulthood.

God intends for parents to take on the incredibly important responsibility of modeling faith and trust for their children, but I'm not so sure many parents today are willing to live their lives as the role models their children need them to be. And that increasingly concerns me.

I'm reminded of a recent conversation I had with a certain man in his early fifties. I've known the gentleman for a long time, and a recent turn of events in his health left him in a difficult situation. No longer able to work, his days were filled with a little too much time to stew over his life-threatening problem.

His mother, sister, and many other relatives died of the same disease he is now battling, and without healing, it appears he will be next. The look on his face told me that the countdown clock to death had begun in his heart.

I sensed he had already started seeing his untimely death as inevitable. His fear was leading him to give up. So as I laid my hands on him to pray, these words came out of my mouth:

Lord, help him to fight, not for his own life necessarily, but for the lives of his children, and their children. Instead of leaving a legacy of this disease, let his life leave a legacy of an amazing miracle.

I gently squeezed his hand, smiled, and walked away. His choice between giving up in fear and determining to fight in faith for healing is his to make. Although there is no way for me to predict the outcome of his struggle, I know this: he must *choose* to fight for his miracle.

Fighting *against* fear and fighting *for* faith is worth the effort, especially in light of all those whom we influence. Sometimes in the midst of grave illness it may be hard to feel as if the fight to stay alive is worth the effort, especially when we know we're going to Heaven when this life is over. But if we'll focus on staying engaged in the battle—however long the battle lasts—it will be worth it.

The fight for faith and against fear will be worth the effort, even if through the battle we have only encouraged others to also trust God and endure the difficulties that come their way.

So, how do we begin to successfully fight for what the Word of God says is ours, and fight for those who are looking to us as examples? First and foremost, our understanding of God's goodness and His great love for us must be solidified.

My daughter recently read a book by John Stickl,[48] titled *Follow the Cloud*. Inspired by a story in that book, we, as a family, have adopted a faith-boosting ending to our family prayers:

"God is good. He has forgiven me. I am loved. And anything is possible with Him."

My adult children don't necessarily need this verbal reminder at the end of our family prayers since they were raised in a home saturated with faith-filled thoughts, but we are deliberately preparing to train the next generation even before their arrival. Grandchildren will be born in time, and as these life-giving words become engrained in my grandchildren's hearts and minds, their training in faith-

---

48 *Follow the Cloud: Hearing God's Voice One Next Step at a Time*, by John Stickl, published by Multnomah, 2017.

filled thinking will have begun.

Truly believing God's words to us begins with trusting that He is good, that He is the Savior He says He is, that He loves us more than we can ever comprehend, and that all His promises are accessible to us through His Word. I believe children who grow up memorizing and internalizing faith-building statements will be well on their way toward living an incredibly impactful adult life for the Kingdom of God.

However, even if we as adults don't have a rich heritage of faith learned from our families, a life filled with confidence and faith is still available to us. We can still obtain and develop a faith-filled perspective on life by saturating our hearts and minds with the Word of God.

Of course pursuing such a perspective requires us to determine to put forth the effort to allow God's Word to change us. And that can be challenging for the flesh that often tries to limit us in our spiritual pursuits. But as we are changed by the Holy Spirit, we'll find that our responses toward the things we experience will begin lining up with the faith-filled thoughts many of us have always desired.

As we begin living lives saturated with God's Word (with our minds renewed and delivered from fear) we will begin walking forward unafraid. And as we do that—as we face every trial and challenge with faith and confidence—we will find that we are building the endurance we will need for meeting every challenge in the future.

James wrote in his letter about endurance:

Dear brothers and sisters, when troubles of any kind come your way, consider it an opportunity for great joy. For you know that when your faith is tested, your endurance has a chance to grow. So let it grow, for when your endurance is fully developed, you will be perfect and complete, needing nothing. (James 1:2-4)

Being perfect and complete can seem like something that is forever beyond our reach. But when we are full of faith, following close to our Savior, and under His protective shadow, we will *grow toward* Christ's perfection as we become more and more like Him. And because of that, we will grow in confidence and overcome all fear.

With our confidence in God, we declare we *can* live without fear.

The Holy Spirit is actively at work in us to increase our faith, to continually and progressively mold us into God's image, and to walk hand-in-hand with us through every trial. As we endure challenges of all kinds, we will continue to grow stronger in faith and trust. And by continuing to trust in God, we will become even better equipped in the future to, indeed, walk forward unafraid.

CHAPTER 6

Chosen to Shine

I HAVE HEARD the concept of walking through difficult circumstances described as walking through darkness. The figurative lack of light we perceive in the midst of our difficulties can certainly seem like the darkness of the night. In the darkness, confusion can set in because we can't see clearly. And when walking through the darkness of difficult circumstances we can be tempted to think that our circumstances might not improve.

But anytime darkness is dispelled by light, everything changes. Night becomes day; perspectives shift; paths become illuminated. That's what happens when God's light is shined into our lives and the lives of others. I don't think we Christians always realize the potential power we possess to bring Christ's life-giving light into the world around us. It's as if we walk through our lives with an untapped reservoir of enormous light-filled power within us that doesn't get out.

The world around us needs the light we have to share. But it's so easy for us to go about our days caught up in our daily routines seemingly unaware of our access to this potential power. Even in our devotion time with the Lord we can rush through it by reading perhaps only one verse and call it done. With so little time set aside to truly sit in the Lord's presence, we can easily begin to lose perspective and not only fail to share light with others but also begin seeing our own situations through the darkness of a worldly mindset.

When that happens, material objects can begin taking priority over spiritual things; quick replies can take the place of Spirit-led responses; completion of personal tasks can become more important than focusing on the needs of others. And before we realize it's happened, we can become guilty of no longer walking in the Spirit's power and loving the people around us. Consequently, lives once so useful in the Kingdom lose their primary purpose of representing God and blend in with other lives that have become ineffective in impacting the world for Jesus.

Just as God called His children out of Egypt long ago to represent Him to the world, we are still called to walk with that same purpose today. The apostle Peter reminds us:

. . . you are a chosen people. You are royal priests, a holy
nation, God's very own possession. As a result, you can
show others the goodness of God, for he called you out of
the darkness into his wonderful light. (1 Peter 2:9)

We, as Christians, have been chosen to represent Christ
and His kingdom. And that is for the purpose of showing
others the goodness of God. We have been called out of
darkness into His *"wonderful light"* so we might lead others
into that same light. In other words, we have been *chosen to
shine* as we reflect His light.

But just because we have been chosen for that work
doesn't mean that we automatically or consistently devote
ourselves to it. If we ask ourselves why, we may obtain
insight into the causes of our lack of devotion.

Perhaps we're simply lazy. Perhaps we spend too much
time trying to meet our own needs. Or perhaps our light
has dimmed because we've muddied our lives with what we
might think is *acceptable sin.* Of course no sin is acceptable to
God, but the tendency to compromise God's instructions to
us is part of the effects of the sin nature into which we were
born. We must recognize and battle against it.

When we receive the salvation that Jesus purchased for
us, our *rebirth* in the Spirit brings to us a new awareness
of our need to adhere to God's instructions. Our pursuit of
doing so leads us toward growing in holiness as we become

more like Christ. God calls His followers to holiness, and according to Scripture it is not an option. It is also not for the weak or double minded.

Peter addressed the importance of holiness when he wrote to his brothers and sisters:

> But now you must be holy in everything you do, just as God who chose you is holy. For the Scriptures say, "You must be holy because I am holy." (1 Peter 1:15-16)

In this Scripture, Peter referred to what was written in the book of Leviticus. The book of Leviticus is full of detailed laws and standards by which Israel would be judged as they dwelled in the Land of Promise. In giving His people instructions, God stated three separate times that He expected His people to be holy.

> For I am the LORD your God. You must consecrate yourselves and be holy, because I am holy. . . . For I, the LORD, am the one who brought you up from the land of Egypt, that I might be your God. Therefore, you must be holy because I am holy. (Leviticus 11:44-45)

> Give the following instructions to the entire community of Israel. You must be holy because I, the LORD your God, am holy. (Leviticus 19:2)

So set yourselves apart to be holy, for I am the Lord your God. (Leviticus 20:7)

The nation of Israel existed only because of what God had done for them as He went about fulfilling the promises He made to Abraham. He had every right to place demands on them. But the importance of His requirement for them to be holy went far beyond simply pleasing their Creator and meeting any need they had. Their holiness was meant to point others to God.

In order for His people (us included) to truly represent God and His intentions to the world, they must shine the light they have been given. And the only way we can truly shine as God's representatives is to shine out to the world the light He gives us so others will see Him—so they will see Him in *His* holiness.

The Scriptures tell us that to whom much is given, much is required.[49] And we have certainly been given *much*! The prophets of the Old Testament had only a glimpse of God's beautiful plan for their salvation, and ours. To them, in many ways it was a mystery. But because God is not only holy but also dependable, He, step by step, gave to us a full revelation of His great plan for saving all who believe! We

---

49 "But someone who does not know, and then does something wrong, will be punished only lightly. When someone has been given much, much will be required in return; and when someone has been entrusted with much, even more will be required" (Luke 12:48).

now have the privilege of understanding what the prophets only knew in part.

As Peter was writing to the New Testament believers, he reminded them of the wonder of salvation:

> And now this Good News has been announced to you by those who preached in the power of the Holy Spirit sent from heaven. It is all so wonderful that even the angels are eagerly watching these things happen.   (1 Peter 1:12b)

Those who lived in the days prior to the Messiah's arrival looked forward to the time in which those New Testament believers were living. With their privileged position in history in mind, Peter instructed his readers:

> So prepare your minds for action and exercise self-control. Put all your hope in the gracious salvation that will come to you when Jesus Christ is revealed to the world. So you must live as God's obedient children. Don't slip back into your old ways of living to satisfy your own desires. You didn't know any better then. But now you must be holy in everything you do, just as God who chose you is holy. . . .

> For you know that God paid a ransom to save you from the empty life you inherited from your ancestors. And it was not paid with mere gold or silver, which lose their value. It was the precious blood of Christ, the sinless, spotless Lamb of God. God chose him as your ransom long

before the world began, but now in these last days he has
been revealed for your sake. (1 Peter 1:13-15, 18-20)

People often act as if their lives belong only to them—as
if they are theirs to do with as they please. But as Peter so
beautifully penned, we've been ransomed (purchased out of
servitude to sin) with the most precious commodity possible,
the *"precious blood of Christ."* When we allow this truth to
sink deep down into our hearts, we should begin to see our
lives differently. Out of overwhelming gratitude, we should
not only recognize our value to Him but submit to Him and
allow *His* greatest purpose to be carried out through us—that
is, to draw all humankind to Him.

This knowledge should cause us to ask: Are our lives
truly beacons of His light? Is His grace and His mercy upheld
through our lives for all to see? And, if we're honest with
this, it's time for further self-examination! We should begin
asking ourselves more questions such as:

"Am I walking in love?"

"Am I dealing with temptation according to God's
Word?"

"Am I filled up with the Word and praying with
expectation?"

"Am I living with eternal perspective?"

As we become focused on Christ, His Word, His Church,
and His purpose, our lives burst forth with His light. Here is
one of my favorite verses concerning Christ's light:

If you are filled with light, with no dark corners, then your whole life will be radiant, as though a floodlight were filling you with light. (Luke 11:36)

Being filled with His light requires purposeful effort on our part; it requires a passionate pursuit of Christ. We must become more like Him, but the effort it takes to become more like Him, to walk in holiness, is contrary to the self-focus of human nature. We must *actively* persevere.

It seems that simply walking out our daily lives on Earth reminds us of our fallen nature. And it takes no extra effort on our part to be exposed to the darkness of sinful humanity that exists all around us. As we continue our pursuit of Christ, if we are to be different, if we are to reflect His transforming light, then we must reject that darkness and immerse ourselves in Him.

Matthew wrote these words of Jesus delivered in what we call His *Sermon on the Mount*:

You are the light of the world—like a city on a hilltop that cannot be hidden. No one lights a lamp and then puts it under a basket. Instead, a lamp is placed on a stand, where it gives light to everyone in the house. In the same way, let

your good deeds shine out for all to see, so that everyone
will praise your heavenly Father. (Matthew 5:14-16)

We understand that Jesus is actually the ultimate Light that shines in the world.[50] Without *Him* there would be nothing but darkness in the world. But Jesus made a point of emphasizing that His followers also are *"the light of the world."* I believe this is true only because we have the ability to reflect *His* light. And we can do that only when we are *in the Lord*—when we dwell in Him—just as Jesus was in the Father. Clearly that is how it is supposed to be.[51]

As we learn to walk in holiness, our light—His light—shines through our actions.

Our ability to be *the light of the world* has everything to do with how close we are to God and how our faith demonstrates that through our actions. Our actions prove whether or not we are actually *in* Christ.[52] And our existence as a light shining in the world will be demonstrated only

---

50 "Jesus spoke to the people once more and said, 'I am the light of the world. If you follow me, you won't have to walk in darkness, because you will have the light that leads to life'" (John 8:12).

51 "I am praying not only for these disciples but also for all who will ever believe in me through their message. I pray that they will all be one, just as you and I are one—as you are in me, Father, and I am in you. And may they be in us so that the world will believe you sent me" (John 17:20-21).

52 "Remain in me, and I will remain in you. For a branch cannot produce fruit if it is severed from the vine, and you cannot be fruitful unless you remain in me. Yes, I am the vine; you are the branches. Those who remain in me, and I in them, will produce much fruit. For apart from me you can do nothing" (John 15:4-5).

when our actions show that we are indeed His and living under His approval. James, the brother of Jesus, wrote:

> Don't you remember that our ancestor Abraham was shown to be right with God by his actions when he offered his son Isaac on the altar? You see, his faith and actions worked together. His actions made his faith complete. And so it happened just as the Scriptures say:
>
> "Abraham believed God, and God counted him as righteous because of his faith."
>
> He was even called the friend of God. So you see, we are shown to be right with God by what we do, not by faith alone.
>
> Rahab the prostitute is another example. She was shown to be right with God by her actions when she hid those messengers and sent them safely away by a different road. Just as the body is dead without breath, so also faith is dead without good works.   (James 2:21-26)

Through his writing, James is telling us that our actions prove what is in our hearts. We are not made right with God *because* of our good deeds; we are made right with God through faith alone. But true faith is evident through a changed heart that produces right attitudes, life-giving words, and good deeds.

True faith involves a commitment of our whole selves to God by choosing to align our hearts and our lives with God's Word. That's not always easy to do. But as we learn to trust God and desire to please Him, we know that He will give us the power to prove our faith through our lives.

Following the reasoning of James, Abraham trusted God so much that he was willing to do whatever God told him to do. Abraham's actions proved he trusted God. And the acts of Rahab the prostitute proved that she trusted God, too.

When Joshua planned the conquest of Jericho, he sent spies to investigate the fortifications of the city. The spies met a woman named Rahab, who under normal circumstances would not likely receive much in the way of spiritual support from God's people. She was both a Gentile and a prostitute living in the city God was about to destroy. But she showed faith in God by helping the spies, and as a result, she and her family were saved. Rahab proved her faith in God by her actions. Faith inspires and leads us to do what is right. And our obedience demonstrates that our faith is genuine.

But James goes on to say that it's not just our actions that either prove or disprove the reality of our faith. The words we say do the same.

> *If you claim to be religious but don't control your tongue, you are fooling yourself, and your religion is worthless.*
>
> (James 1:26)

People can tame all kinds of animals, birds, reptiles, and fish, but no one can tame the tongue. It is restless and evil, full of deadly poison. Sometimes it praises our Lord and Father, and sometimes it curses those who have been made in the image of God. And so blessing and cursing come pouring out of the same mouth. Surely, my brothers and sisters, this is not right! (James 3:7-10)

We should never be careless with our tongues. Although we may not be able to perfectly control our tongues at all times, they should never have a reputation of being out of control. The Holy Spirit will help us learn how to control the words we speak; we must allow Him to do so.

We have a choice every time we open our mouths. We can speak encouragement and life, or we can speak destruction and death. And without doubt, if a person is continually speaking destruction and death, that person is in serious spiritual trouble. That person reveals darkness, not light, by his or her own words.

God gave us the opportunity to create a life-giving atmosphere with our words. We can comfort others with our words. We can encourage people with our words. We can give direction to the lost and the saved alike with our words. But our tongues must continually be under the watchful care and direction of the Holy Spirit; because if they aren't, if we're not careful, our tongues can yield themselves to gossiping, bragging, putting others down, and complaining.

Before we speak, we must ask ourselves: "Is what I want to say truthful? Is it kind? Is it necessary?"

Not everything we *want* to say *needs* to be said. A man I know and greatly respect, wisely prays, "Lord, help me to leave more unsaid than spoken." If we do that, it will be a clear demonstration of self-control in our lives.

The Psalmist, David, wrote these words:

May the words of my mouth and the meditation of my heart be pleasing to you, O LORD, my rock and my redeemer. (Psalm 19:14)

Before the words leave our mouths, we can and should choose what we're going to say. That also includes words we write, such as in e-mail messages and on social media. Once our words are heard or read, we cannot make people forget them. Just like a fire that spreads quickly and does enormous damage, our poorly chosen words can cause widespread destruction. It is better we choose to be quiet than to let destructive words come out of our mouths.

If you are wise and understand God's ways, prove it by living an honorable life, doing good works with the humility that comes from wisdom. (James 3:13)

We choose to show our faith by speaking good words and doing good works with humility. Being able to live a life of goodness and possessing His life-giving light is our reward.

By exhibiting understanding and wisely living in His light, we are pleasing to God, our Father, and we become His light to people living in darkness.

Regardless of whether we are using our actions or our words to positively affect other people and lead them into God's kingdom, or disciple those who already dwell in it, we followers of Christ are the ones chosen to shine, and who are suited for the task.

Illuminate the world. Dispel the darkness. Shine brightly!

CHAPTER 7

Strategically Positioned

IN EVER-WIDENING CIRCLES, our lives make an impact on those we influence—either positively or negatively. How we live matters. And a life that is expressed in faith-filled deeds and hope-filled words is the heritage that followers of Christ should aspire to pass on to those around them.

Those who live among us and follow us in life are watching the way we live. And by simply living before them we are positioned to influence their futures; we are inviting them to pattern their lives after ours. This certainly includes our own children.

Parents are positioned to affect their children's lives forever. And Christian parents desire to prepare their children to live with godly, mature perspectives and attitudes in a world that doesn't always share our foundation on the Word of God.

As parents raise their children, they usually have markers in mind that they use to track their children's growth. (Here, I'm not talking about marks on a doorframe to track their growth in height. I'm referring to tracking growth in their children's levels of maturity.) But for each family, these growth markers may look different depending on the family's value system.

Some parents might believe that age itself provides the mark of maturity, and when their children are eighteen they are automatically deemed mature adults. Other parents might use entry into the workplace as the mark of maturity they anticipate. If so, they may declare that when their children become full-time wage earners they have arrived at their place in society as mature adults.

For me, recognizing godly living in speech and deed has always been high on my list of indicators of maturity. Indicators that might be considered less often by others, but have proven insightful to me as a parent encouraging maturity in my children, are the words spoken from my children's hearts in prayer.

Quoting Jesus, Luke wrote:

A good person produces good things from the treasury of a good heart, and an evil person produces evil things from

> *the treasury of an evil heart. What you say flows from*
> *what is in your heart.*   (Luke 6:45)

With this truth in mind, I listened to my children's spoken prayers with great interest during their *growing-up* years.

As my children were growing up it was important to me to model for them what it was like to pray sincerely with an open heart before God. We prayed together as a family on the way to school, before meals, in thanksgiving for God's goodness, and in times of crisis or major decision. In other words, we prayed a lot.

Teaching my children to approach prayer with childlike trust—to rely on the full strength of their heavenly Father's faithfulness and love—was one of my most important goals. Occasionally, I asked them to pray out loud, and I listened with joy as their tender hearts openly connected with their Heavenly Father. As they grew older and their ability to read and understand the Word of God grew, their prayers grew, too. Their prayers matured in both boldness and insight into God's character and nature.

My youngest child, nearly twenty-two now, prayed during our family dinner last week; and my heart soared as I listened to his words of bold petition, thanksgiving, and obvious devotion. As I sensed he had reached a new level of maturity in his understanding of God's character and nature, I quietly said in my heart, "He's ready now."

We tend to pass on to others who we've become. So partly for my children's sake, but also for my own, I'm grateful I am continuing to develop a greater understanding of God's character and my identity in Him as *His* child. As we pursue knowing the Lord and growing in Him, He reveals more of himself to us, and He continues to prove His faithfulness to us as we seek to serve Him.

But we ourselves were once children watching and responding to our own parents and others whom God positioned to affect our lives. We should be grateful for the lives they lived before us. In his letter, Peter reminded his readers of their heritage as the children of those who faithfully and honorably served God in previous generations.

Sarah was one of those people. Her life became an example of living a life of honor before others as she obeyed her husband and demonstrated the inner beauty of a submissive heart.

> *Don't be concerned about the outward beauty of fancy hairstyles, expensive jewelry, or beautiful clothes. You should clothe yourselves instead with the beauty that comes from within, the unfading beauty of a gentle and quiet spirit, which is so precious to God. This is how the holy women of old made themselves beautiful. They put their trust in God and accepted the authority of their husbands. For instance, Sarah obeyed her husband,*

Abraham, and called him her master. You are her
daughters when you do what is right without fear of
what your husbands might do.   (1 Peter 3:3-6)

Sarah's humble submission became a mark of maturity among all believers. And all of Christ's followers—both male and female—can emulate Sarah's example of living a life of obedience and humility as we seek to correctly position our hearts before God and those in authority over us.

Peter followed his words about Sarah by counseling husbands in verse seven to treat their wives with honor. Showing honor to those around us, especially members of our family is another mark of maturity. Then Peter went on to write:

Finally, all of you should be of one mind. Sympathize
with each other. Love each other as brothers and sisters. Be
tenderhearted, and keep a humble attitude. (1 Peter 3:8)

Through our godly example of holy living demonstrated by humble submission, by showing sympathy for others who experience needs and weaknesses, by loving and honoring each other, and by being tenderhearted toward one another in an attitude of humility, we impact another generation for His kingdom.

We tend to wonder sometimes whether our lives are making a difference, but if we are truly living for God, we will look back on our lives one day from the perspective of heaven and rejoice over how God took something as insignificant as our short lifespans and used them to impact humanity for His glory.

Think of this: All our heroes of faith whose lives were recorded in Scripture did not just affect the lives of the people around them. They did not just affect the family members who followed them in life. And they did not just affect those who first read about them in the Old Testament, or those who first read the words that Peter and the others penned in the New Testament. They still affect our lives today. Lives well lived in God's approval so many years ago continue to affect multitudes of people who continue to read and understand God's Word today.

Somehow, as the Lord strategically positions His followers to fulfill their purposes in the Kingdom, God weaves our lives together like a tapestry, spanning generations, to create a beautiful story of His grace and power.

Several years ago, my grandfather gave me a notebook of our family's genealogy. It's filled with unfamiliar names and people whose lives somehow providentially intersected over many years. Among the pages of the family tree was a note written by the mother of my mom's first cousin. The note referenced my great, great grandmother.

My great, great grandmother was known as *Momma Wallace.* It turns out that she was a woman preacher long before it was generally acceptable for women to stand in the pulpit. Also included in the correspondence was a copy of her only remaining sermon, which is titled *The Woman's Part: Her Right to Preach.*

Her sermon was passed to me, and as I read through it, I thought back on the number of times I've had to defend God's mandate on *my* life to proclaim His message. Then I thought back farther to the struggles my mother encountered as an ordained minister. She was frequently, verbally reprimanded for her audacity to believe that she, as a woman, had been called by God to be a preacher.

My mom's mother—my grandmother—faithfully led many people to Christ over the course of many years during her summertime *Happy Day Club* for the children of her Santa Barbara, California neighborhood.

And *her* mother? I don't know her story. I had the privilege of sitting in her presence only once in my young life. But I do know that she married the son of Momma Wallace, my preaching ancestor!

There's something incredibly satisfying about knowing that I'm *at home* in my genealogy. My genealogy somehow welcomes me and makes me feel comfortable in my calling. I'm so thankful for the effect the lives of my predecessors have had on my life and ministry.

I find myself wondering who might have influenced Momma Wallace. I may never know the answer this side of heaven. But what I do know is that her act of obedience to preach God's Word set in motion generations of women who *have* answered, *are* answering, and *will* answer the call of God on their lives.

Answering God's call begins with humble surrender to God's will, and after the call is answered it is often marked by moments of reassuring transformation along the way. God has given me many such moments over the years, and I'm grateful. One particular moment stands out in my memory:

I had the privilege once of meeting Andy Andrews, speaker and author of many books, including *The Butterfly Effect*. As I stood next to him smiling for a picture, I couldn't help but think I was standing in one of those transformational moments in my life. But it really had little to do with who Andy Andrews was. I felt impressed by the moment because something in my world was shifting.

At the time, I had only just begun the journey of seeing my writing published, speaking at conferences, preaching in pulpits, developing a business, going through training to become a certified life coach, and considering the daunting task of pulling all of my activities and ministries together into a nonprofit organization.

The courage I needed in my life to keep trudging through the unfamiliar territory of what has since become simply *adventurous living* was enormous. Yet I knew I could never do less than keep giving my best effort, even in the face of the unknown. I was raised that way.

God's Word provided me with so many heroic examples of people who had likewise walked adventurous paths. My time spent in God's Word over the years created for me a world of heroes like Abraham, Moses, Joshua, Deborah, David, Paul, Peter, James, and of course Jesus. The biblical examples of perseverance and godliness that I saw in them became models for my own transformation into what I hope has become a fitting example for others to follow.

But beyond all those heroes of the Bible and so many others who lived and faithfully ministered throughout Church history leading up to today, I had the examples of members of my own family to provide encouragement to me. I didn't overlook the strength and courage they exhibited before me. Regardless of the decades or centuries in which they pursued their own callings, their faith and courage instilled confidence in me.

As I thanked Mr. Andrews for our brief photo opportunity, he handed me his book, *The Butterfly Effect*. I'd heard the story, but it would be almost two years before I picked up the book again and read through it.

As I read the book I saw myself in his words. I read:

> There are generations yet unborn whose very lives will be shifted and shaped by the moves you make and the actions you take today. And tomorrow. And the next day. And the next. Every single thing you do matters. [53]

The assurance that the value of the investments we make today will be borne out in future tomorrows makes our courageous push forward worth any effort.

Adventurous living recently yielded yet another transformational opportunity in and through my life:

There is a pastor with whom I collaborate in international ministry. He lives in Pakistan. He recently asked me to begin a Bible school for young adult men and women (teaching by video conferencing). They are so hungry to grow in God's Word and in ministry.

How beautiful to experience that!

I agreed to conduct the classes and went about making arrangements. The classes have started now. And in the

---

53 From *The Butterfly Effect: How Your Life Matters*, by Andy Andrews, published by Simple Truths, LLC, 2009.

early stages of this new ministry I can't stop wondering who I'm influencing and *how* I'm influencing them as I allow the Holy Spirit to use me to prepare the students for ministry in Pakistan and beyond.

To be perfectly honest with you, it's not convenient for me to do this work. Because of the time difference between here and Pakistan, I'm up before the sun rises most Tuesday mornings. While my neighbors and family members are sleeping, I'm up, dressed, and teaching Bible students half a world away.

But don't feel sorry for me, because I have a choice in the matter. No, I can't choose another time to teach, but I can choose to not do it. But then again, I don't believe I actually could choose sleep over equipping a young generation of Pakistani witnesses for Christ. So I guess you can say that I don't really have a choice after all.

But perhaps it would be more accurate for me to say that I *willingly* don't have a choice.

What I have just said will make perfect sense to a lot of people who have already answered God's call and dedicated themselves to making a difference in the lives of others. How could I possibly pass up an opportunity to serve my Lord in such a powerful way? The Lord has positioned me and is enabling me to influence the next generation in ways I previously could not have imagined.

We make decisions each moment of every day; and some of those decisions are between convenience and influence— between choosing to remain conveniently satisfied with our comfort or launching out in some endeavor to influence people with our actions and words. We might enjoy our convenience, but others will appreciate and benefit from our influence.

When properly applied, godly influence lays the foundation on which a good legacy is built. I'm grateful to have descended from a long line of godly influencers—those who have chosen legacy over comfort. But it's incredibly reassuring to know that God will begin today, at this moment, to accept and equip anyone (even if they have no such legacy) who will choose to take up the responsibility of influencing others to benefit His kingdom.

As I sit writing this morning, I'm listening to the birds happily chirping outside my office window. It's early spring, which makes the warmer, more summerlike weather a bit of an oddity here in Nashville. A newness, a hope for the beauty of spring, is stirring in my heart. Our Lord is a God of new beginnings and new seasons. That's especially good news for those who don't have a heritage of a purposeful, godly legacy.

Perhaps you're the first in your family to believe on Jesus Christ. That gives you the opportunity to make *your* life the beginning of a *brand new* legacy. God longs to use you for building a godly legacy for your family and others your life will touch both now and in the future. Your life matters. Lived for God, your life will be used to lead others to be full of faith and courage. But every moment from here forward requires your deliberate focus on making that happen.

Imagine what your grandchildren's lives might look like as they grow up knowing Jesus and walk with Him into their adult years. Life-draining addictions don't plague them. Freedom in Christ grants them the ability to dream forward and invest their lives in His kingdom. You witness your children and grandchildren reaching glorious markers of maturity in Christ as they learn to serve Him. That is what God wants for you and your descendants as you move forward after a fresh new start as a legacy builder.

My mind drifts toward the book of Jeremiah as I ponder the newness of a fresh start. The people of Judah, God's people, had been exiled to Babylon because of their grievous sins and unrepentant hearts.

> *...for they have deserted me; they burn incense to worthless idols. They have stumbled off the ancient highways and walk in muddy paths.* (Jeremiah 18:15)

God passed judgment upon them, and they were sentenced to serve another master—one much less loving than their heavenly Father had proven himself to be to them. But God's punishment wasn't intended to cast them away from His presence forever; it was meant to bring their hearts back to Him. God assured the exiles in Babylon that He would bring them home to their beloved Jerusalem after they spent a full seventy years in captivity.[54]

> *I will watch over and care for them, and I will bring them back here again. I will build them up and not tear them down. I will plant them and not uproot them. I will give them hearts that recognize me as the LORD. They will be my people, and I will be their God, for they will return to me wholeheartedly.* (Jeremiah 24:6-7)

God's comforting words of restoration are rather amazing when we consider the depth of their sin. And yet, that's the incredible beauty of who God is. He is not only the God of new beginnings, He is *the Restorer.*

When I consider God as both *the Restorer* and *God of new beginnings*, I am particularly moved by a passage in Jeremiah chapter thirty-one. In the words recorded by Jeremiah prior to the passage quoted below, God's words to the people anticipate what it will be like when those in

---

54 "This is what the LORD says: 'You will be in Babylon for seventy years. But then I will come and do for you all the good things I have promised, and I will bring you home again'" (Jeremiah 29:10).

exile call out in repentance and return home to Him. He speaks of their prosperity, their joy, and their shared love as they are restored to right living and respectful fellowship with God.

Then, during God's discourse, His words shift from talking about the Jews being restored to their land to talking about establishing a "new covenant" with them. Instead of just speaking of the restoration of His children to Jerusalem, He rejoices over a new covenant that is signified by His laws, or instructions, being written on the hearts of men.

> *"The day is coming," says the LORD, "when I will make a new covenant with the people of Israel and Judah. This covenant will not be like the one I made with their ancestors when I took them by the hand and brought them out of the land of Egypt. They broke that covenant, though I loved them as a husband loves his wife," says the LORD.*

> *"But this is the new covenant I will make with the people of Israel after those days," says the LORD. "I will put my instructions deep within them, and I will write them on their hearts. I will be their God, and they will be my people."*   (Jeremiah 31:31-33)

Far more can be said of the new covenant than space will allow here, but to put it succinctly, the new covenant speaks of the salvation and relationship we have with God that is made possible only by the birth and ministry of Jesus, His sacrifice, and His resurrection.[55]

Oh, the beauty of those words! What an amazing, saving, restoring, God of new beginnings we serve! As we consider our own lives, situations, and genealogies in light of the gift of our Savior and how He has worked in our families and circles of influence, we are assured that God is ready to begin doing a new thing anywhere He is given the opportunity to do so.

Generations yet to be influenced by our godly example lie ahead of us. And you and I have been strategically positioned in this moment of time for the purpose of carrying forward a heritage of godliness—or perhaps initiating and setting in motion a new one—through our humble submission to our Lord and to one another.

Let's lay hold of our opportunity and make the most it!

---

55 "As they were eating, Jesus took some bread and blessed it. Then he broke it in pieces and gave it to the disciples, saying, 'Take this and eat it, for this is my body.' And he took a cup of wine and gave thanks to God for it. He gave it to them and said, 'Each of you drink from it, for this is my blood, which confirms the covenant between God and his people. It is poured out as a sacrifice to forgive the sins of many'" (Matthew 26:26-28).

CHAPTER 8

Inspired by Hope

THE CHALLENGES WE face in life have a way of pushing us, pressuring us, and closing in on us. And sometimes challenges that come our way can threaten to hold us back from accomplishing what God has planned for our lives. We can be tempted to give into challenges and accept the limits they try to put on us. But the beauty of restoration and the hope of new beginnings motivate us to move forward through life's challenges and difficulties.

I rejoice each time I see someone conquer life's challenges, but especially when a person overcomes a potentially overwhelming difficulty. In Christian circles we commonly call such people *overcomers*. A man named Roger Crawford is one of those.

Roger was born in 1960 with one finger on his right hand and two on his left. Roger's right foot has three toes, and his lower left leg was amputated when he was only five years old. Associating the name Roger Crawford with the title of *professional athlete* and member of the United States Professional Tennis Association probably seemed impossible as that baby boy entered the world. Yet this is only one of the many titles conferred on him today.

In Roger's early years, his parents apparently chose to see his disability as simply a difficulty to overcome. They encouraged him to not let his disability hold him back from anything he chose to pursue. No one would disagree with the fact that learning to play tennis in a competitive environment is often a real challenge for even a non-disabled person, but almost no one in Roger's life would have believed it possible for him.

For many who knew Roger there seemed to be no hope for him to accomplish what he did. And truthfully, where hope doesn't exist, there can be no expectation of success. But hope existed for Roger's parents, and their hope was instilled in Roger. Roger was driven to succeed because of that hope, and success was exactly what he experienced.

This illustrates what I believe to be a powerful principle of hope: It doesn't take an army of people to believe in you for you to be a success in what you do; just one or two strategically positioned encouragers can spark the flame of hope needed to motivate you to rise above your circumstances

Roger did what no one expected he could. He possessed hope, and it inspired him. Roger chose to rise above his difficulties. Today Roger is a motivational speaker, and he is using the results of his choice to influence others. By sharing his experiences and encouraging others, he has sparked a sense of hope in many people who hear his story.

Roger now says, "I think what holds people back most often is self-imposed limitations."[56]

There were people who had their doubts about Roger's pursuits. But Roger persevered and ignored their hopeless outlooks. And today, by Roger's own words, he releases even the smallest amount of blameworthiness from the naysayers in his life.

Although it would be easier to blame others for our lack of opportunity or success, we often don't realize that we can be guilty of creating our own personal limitations that grow out of our own lack of hope. We must never allow anyone to dissuade us from having hope. But we should also never allow ourselves to develop attitudes of hopelessness due to our own lack of faith and trust in God.

---

56 From Roger's *YouTube* video: https://www.youtube.com/watch?v=K5t4d18T_-I. See also: http://www.tennis.com/pro-game/2017/10/roger-crawford-heroes-tennis-channel-2017/69908/

The apostle Peter began his letter to his fellow believers with words that encouraged them to have an eternal, hope-filled perspective. According to Peter, the trials those believers were facing were going to prove to have been beneficial— more precious than gold—on the day when they would stand before Christ in all His glory.

All praise to God, the Father of our Lord Jesus Christ. It is by his great mercy that we have been born again, because God raised Jesus Christ from the dead. Now we live with great expectation, and we have a priceless inheritance— an inheritance that is kept in heaven for you, pure and undefiled, beyond the reach of change and decay. And through your faith, God is protecting you by his power until you receive this salvation, which is ready to be revealed on the last day for all to see.

So be truly glad. There is wonderful joy ahead, even though you must endure many trials for a little while. These trials will show that your faith is genuine. It is being tested as fire tests and purifies gold—though your faith is far more precious than mere gold. So when your faith remains strong through many trials, it will bring you much praise and glory and honor on the day when Jesus Christ is revealed to the whole world.

You love him even though you have never seen him. Though you do not see him now, you trust him; and you rejoice with a glorious, inexpressible joy. The reward for trusting him will be the salvation of your souls.

(1 Peter 1:3-9)

We must not allow our challenges and difficulties to take away the hope we have in Christ. Challenges and difficulties try us. But God will use those trials to purify our faith; and recognizing that should make our hope thrive as we increase our trust in God and look forward to receiving hope's beautiful reward. We indeed look forward with *great confidence* to our reward for trusting Him.

As we look at our own life's circumstances from an eternal perspective, we are much better equipped to overcome our challenges. Hope inspires us to rise above our difficulties. Our perspectives shift when we trust God in the pursuit of what we hope for, and in that shift we often discover the answers to our dilemmas.

When I think of the concept of overcoming challenges through the inspiration of hope—hope that leads us into God's power—I am reminded of the Old Testament story of David and Goliath. In the days of King Saul the Israelites were in conflict with the Philistines. The children of God found themselves face to face on the battlefield with that pagan people, and the Philistines were led by their hero, the giant, Goliath.

Chapter seventeen of the first book of Samuel records the tiring, daily taunts of Goliath against God's children. God had demonstrated His care for the Israelites and His power to deliver them for many years. One would think they would be full of faith in God and welcome the chance to see God defend the honor of His name. But instead, they had adopted the perspective of a victim, and they cowered in fear every time Goliath taunted them.

The Israelites surely should have known better! But not so unlike them, it can be easy for us, too, to get so focused on our circumstances that the solutions to our challenges seem elusive. What the fear-filled children of Israel needed was a different perspective, a perspective of hope. And through God's faithfulness, hope indeed showed up in the form of a shepherd named David.

I imagine that no one among Israel's fighting men expected their hero to be a young man who had never fought in a war, and whose life experience still seemed to consist mostly of caring for his father's flocks. But God has a way of using the most unlikely of us to accomplish His miracles. And a miracle is exactly what Israel needed that day.

It appears that David spent much of his childhood in the fields taking care of his father's sheep. Being a shepherd can be a lonely job that affords little contact with other people for long periods of time. But we can assume that in those fields, alone with the sheep, as David grew older he also became more aware of God's continual presence with him. It was in the fields where David must have learned that he could depend on God's power to lead and protect him just like his sheep could depend on him.

It was through his most precious friendship with God while serving as a shepherd that David developed the hope-filled faith he needed to take on the giant. He had trained his ear to hear God's words of encouragement and instruction in the quiet of the pasture. And while protecting the sheep in his care—and in circumstances where being able to depend on God's help became a matter of his own life and death—David honed his skills with the slingshot and the club.

The lion and the bear had met their match in David. And Goliath was next.[57]

David's world had been filled with consistent encouragement and instruction from God, and David seemed certain of his success against Goliath. I'm rather impressed with David's boldness as revealed by Samuel's words about the incident:

---

57 1 Samuel 17:37.

David asked the soldiers standing nearby, "What will a man get for killing this Philistine and ending his defiance of Israel? Who is this pagan Philistine anyway, that he is allowed to defy the armies of the living God?"

But when David's oldest brother, Eliab, heard David talking to the men, he was angry. "What are you doing around here anyway?" he demanded. "What about those few sheep you're supposed to be taking care of? I know about your pride and deceit. You just want to see the battle!"

"What have I done now?" David replied. "I was only asking a question!"

Then David's question was reported to King Saul, and the king sent for him.

"Don't worry about this Philistine," David told Saul. "I'll go fight him!"

"Don't be ridiculous!" Saul replied. "There's no way you can fight this Philistine and possibly win! You're only a boy, and he's been a man of war since his youth."

(1 Samuel 17:26, 28-29, 31-33)

Moving confidently toward the giant—whom not one of his own countrymen who were considered brave warriors would even *attempt* to defeat—David strode right past both his brother's derogatory remarks and King Saul's objections.

I love David's trust in God!

He picked up five smooth stones from a stream and put them into his shepherd's bag. Then, armed only with his shepherd's staff and sling, he started across the valley to fight the Philistine. (1 Samuel 17:40)

Despite Goliath's sneering words, David shouted his boast in the Lord and ran quickly toward the giant with the sling in his hand. Fear had no place in David's heart that day. One stone, one shot . . . sudden victory.

Reaching into his shepherd's bag and taking out a stone, he hurled it with his sling and hit the Philistine in the forehead. The stone sank in, and Goliath stumbled and fell face down on the ground. So David triumphed over the Philistine with only a sling and a stone, for he had no sword. Then David ran over and pulled Goliath's sword from its sheath. David used it to kill him and cut off his head. (1 Samuel 17:49-51)

David didn't hesitate to finish the job completely. And the Philistines fled when they saw their hero was dead.[58]

To his fellow countrymen, David appeared naïve and unprepared; but in fact, he had been trained in the fields by God himself, and he was more prepared than all the others. David was able to see the conflict from God's perspective—

---

58 1 Samuel 17:51.

knowing that what seemed impossible to others was possible with God.

And David didn't allow criticism to stop him. While the rest of the army was frozen in fear, David took action. His primary focus was walking in God's purpose, and he let nothing stand in his way.

What we can learn from David's experience to apply to our own lives seems irresistibly obvious. Are we cultivating hope in our own lives by spending more time listening to God's voice (the voice that will lead us toward our success) rather than the voices that warn of or predict our defeat? Have we trained our ear to listen intently for God's encouragement and trained our attitude to be that of an overcomer?

It seemed everyone else on the battlefield that day—David's own brothers, the other soldiers, and even the king—saw a giant too big for any individual to defeat. David, however, saw a giant too big to miss. With a staff, a slingshot, and five smooth stones in hand, and with faith and hope overflowing his heart, he did the work of a mighty warrior.

How is it that we are tempted to go from reading God's hope-filled words of faith recorded for us in His Word to running in fear from our obstacles? God has faithfully spoken His words over us:

> *You can pray for anything, and if you have faith, you will receive it.* (Matthew 21:22)

> *Anything is possible if a person believes.* (Mark 9:23b)

> *Yes, ask me for anything in my name, and I will do it!* (John 14:14)

Since we are armed with God's truth spoken so boldly over us, what prevents us from overcoming our obstacles and reaching our potential? Could it be that we're simply focused more on our circumstances than on God's truth?

Keeping an eternal perspective and trusting God's Word positions us to proceed with hope-filled belief that God will faithfully accomplish His purposes through our lives. When we lose sight of our eternal focus and the authority of the words contained in Scripture, our hope diminishes, and we become focused on our difficulties.

Hope from a fully Christian perspective means much more than just *hoping against hope* to gain a preferred outcome. It implies an *expectation* of obtaining the good outcome we not only desire but also anticipate. Without receiving inspiration from this hope, people tend to doubt that God will intervene or carry them through their difficulties. And such doubt can lead us into unbelief, which is the mortal enemy of hope.

As a matter of fact, unbelief is such a powerful foe that it caused an entire generation of Israelites to miss out on the blessings God had planned for them.

With the Promised Land in front of them, and Egypt behind them, the children of Israel were instructed to walk forward to possess the land promised to them. There were giants who lived in the land, but even though that might have been a very scary prospect, the Israelites were to trust God and go into the land with their hearts full of hope and confidence.

That Land was the very land promised to Abraham and his family who succeeded him. They should have been thrilled and full of faith. But instead they focused their minds on the difficulties rather than on the One who delivered them from Egypt and parted the waters for them in the face of their enemies. They refused any inspiration that hope could provide to them, and they refused to cross over Jordan.

God's faithfulness insured their protection, deliverance from their formidable opponents, and rest in the land of their inheritance. Their part in taking possession of the land was simply to believe that God would most certainly fulfill His promise. But they couldn't overcome their own feelings of weakness and fear.

Regretfully, their unbelief became their undoing.

After arriving at the Jordan River, Moses sent twelve spies—one from each tribe of the Israelites—across the river and into the Land of Promise to assess the territory so the Israelites could be better prepared to enter the land. After exploring the Promised Land for forty days, the scouts reported their findings to Moses, Aaron, and the people.

This was their report to Moses:

"We entered the land you sent us to explore, and it is indeed a bountiful country—a land flowing with milk and honey. Here is the kind of fruit it produces. But the people living there are powerful, and their towns are large and fortified. We even saw giants there, the descendants of Anak! The Amalekites live in the Negev, and the Hittites, Jebusites, and Amorites live in the hill country. The Canaanites live along the coast of the Mediterranean Sea and along the Jordan Valley."

But Caleb tried to quiet the people as they stood before Moses. "Let's go at once to take the land," he said. "We can certainly conquer it!"

But the other men who had explored the land with him disagreed. "We can't go up against them! They are stronger than we are!"

So they spread this bad report about the land among the Israelites: "The land we traveled through and explored will devour anyone who goes to live there. All the people we

saw were huge. We even saw giants there, the descendants
of Anak. Next to them we felt like grasshoppers, and that's
what they thought, too!"   (Numbers 13:27-33)

Rather than seeing their situation through the hope-filled perspective of God's promises, they deemed their circumstances impossible to overcome. They refused to put their trust in God to once again go before them as they entered into the land. They succumbed to their unbelief and fear, and God judged them.

God's punishment not only denied them entrance into their inheritance at that moment, but it also sentenced them to wandering in the wilderness outside of the Land of Promise for forty years while the entire generation who refused to enter the land died off. The beautiful land of rest God had prepared specifically for His children became inaccessible to that whole generation, and they never knew the pleasure of living there.

So we see that because of their unbelief they were not able
to enter his rest.   (Hebrews 3:19)

Unbelief, then, became their downfall. They lost their hope of receiving the fulfillment of God's promise. Peter seemed to understand the value of hope and how it worked to inspire faith as revealed in the letter he penned to his comrades in Christ:

*Put all your hope in the gracious salvation that will come
to you when Jesus Christ is revealed to the world.*

(1 Peter 1:13b)

So what is hope worth? As for the Israelites waiting to enter the Promised Land, it could have enriched their lives and brought them many blessings. As for God's children facing the Philistines, the inspiration of hope that existed in one young man, David, brought an amazing victory to them. And for those suffering persecution, hope inspired Peter and his fellow believers to remain focused on their eternal promise throughout their difficulties.

And for us today, hope inspires us to lay hold of every opportunity to overcome anything standing in our way. We continue to put our faith in God and actively trust Him each day to make the impossible possible.

*Jesus looked at them intently and said, "Humanly speaking
it is impossible. But with God everything is possible."*

(Matthew 19:26)

Roger Crawford didn't let his fingers, his toes, or his amputated leg dictate what was either possible or impossible, and neither should we. Hope inspires faith and trust in God and His plan. Let it inspire you!

CHAPTER 9

Boundless Love

THE HOPE THAT inspires us to keep moving forward, ever looking toward the eternal reward of heaven, serves as a constant reminder of God's great love for us. His love for us is complete, and that love has always been—and always will be—God's primary motivation as He interacts with His creation. In fact, God's association with love is so complete and far-reaching that the apostle John actually described God as *being* love.

> *But anyone who does not love does not know God, for God is love.* (1 John 4:8)

God is defined by love—real love; and His love is not only real and complete but also holy, perfect, and just. But to fully understand the scope of God's love, and how love is supposed to operate in the world, we must look beyond mere words and see how God's revelation of love is revealed to us through His actions. And when people examine God's actions, they may be surprised to find out that love isn't always what they had believed it to be.

People often misunderstand love. To many, love is always associated with warm feelings and acceptance. In other words, to them love is simply a pleasant emotion. But the truth is, sometimes the greatest love is not demonstrated in pleasant feelings but, instead, in correction. Sometimes love is revealed in acts of doing hard things that initially foster anything but happy, warm feelings.

If we exhibit the kind of love God has always shared with His creation, our love will indeed be seen in tender love, but it will also be seen in what is commonly spoken of today as *tough love*. If we emulate God's love, the love we exhibit will not be seen only in our tenderness toward others; it will also be seen in our unwillingness to allow the lives of others to be ruined by sin. Real love motivates us to attempt to rescue others from sin's destructive influence.

No demonstration of such holy, just, and perfect love can be more powerfully presented to us than through the sacrificial death of Christ recorded in the New Testament. In it we see both God's passionate and tender love for the world and His demand for justice—for sin to be judged. Jesus, the only person who had no sin of His own, loved us so much that He took our sins upon himself and agreed to carry our death sentences for sinning to the cross.

Christ's death on the cross provides us with a clear picture of God's call for justice and His love working together in concert for us.

> *For this is how God loved the world: He gave his one and only Son, so that everyone who believes in him will not perish but have eternal life.* (John 3:16)

While it's the New Testament that provides to us the full beauty of forgiveness expressed through Christ's sacrificial love, the Old Testament is also replete with examples of God's great love toward His children. And many of those examples are seen through the correction God provided to His people because they broke His laws and disobeyed other instructions He provided to them through His prophets.

People generally don't like laws and limitations placed upon them. And although today we may be tempted to view the Old Testament laws as limiting and harsh, God instituted them for our benefit. Their purpose has always been two-fold: First, they serve as a mirror by which people can see their sinfulness. Second, they point people toward a loving God who is looking out for their best interests.

There is a current trend among many Christians to neglect, even push aside, the Old Testament and disregard its importance for today. But by pushing aside the books of the Old Testament and ignoring God's laws, people who do so will fail to sufficiently grasp all the implications of God's love, and they will fail to see the thread of God's boundless love woven throughout Scripture.

We see in the Old Testament that God didn't wait until Jesus was born to display and offer His love to humankind. From the beginning of time His love for us has always been astounding given our constant propensity to live in opposition to His purposes.

In the Old Testament we come across pronouncements of impending judgment in response to humanity's sinful choices. But even in the midst of those predictions, we also read words of restorative hope as they shine forth and make the wonder of God's love more complete and ever greater.

We're not only instructed but also comforted as we read the words written so long ago. For among the words of judgment we also find words of hope for those being judged—words written out of love. And that inspires us to hope today when we fall prey to our humanity.

I recently reread the books of Isaiah, Jeremiah, Lamentations, and Ezekiel; and I admit that studying these books can be difficult reading. It seems as if judgment is the prevailing theme in all of them, and reading of all that judgment can certainly be depressing. But just as soon as I think that I can't take one more chapter of impending doom while reading these books, I discover a beautiful passage that reveals God's faithful love and grips my heart.

Right in the middle of reading about the terrible judgments, I find myself asking God, "How can you possibly love us this much?"

As I wipe the tears from my eyes, I'm simply overwhelmed by His redemptive intentions and relentless pursuit of personal relationships with us.

And then, returning to reading the text, I cringe as once again I read how God's children yielded to temptation, sinned, and brought God's judgment upon themselves—as they so often did. Despite many prophetic warnings, the children of Israel continued generation after generation to prostitute their hearts to other gods. And with His rebukes continuously unheeded, God ended their downward spiral and brought His judgment upon them.

God's judgments upon them were painful but well deserved.

We, too, can bring upon ourselves painful, but deserved consequences when we sin. The tendency for people to sin did not end when Jesus redeemed us on the cross. And God's tendency to reach out in love to correct people when they do sin—especially His own followers—did not end with the Old Testament. God still judges sin and disobedience today.

And have you forgotten the encouraging words God spoke to you as his children?

He said, "My child, don't make light of the Lord's discipline, and don't give up when he corrects you. For the Lord disciplines those he loves, and he punishes each one he accepts as his child." [59]

As you endure this divine discipline, remember that God is treating you as his own children. Who ever heard of a child who is never disciplined by its father? If God doesn't discipline you as he does all of his children, it means that you are illegitimate and are not really his children at all. Since we respected our earthly fathers who disciplined us, shouldn't we submit even more to the discipline of the Father of our spirits, and live forever?

For our earthly fathers disciplined us for a few years, doing the best they knew how. But God's discipline is always good for us, so that we might share in his holiness. No discipline is enjoyable while it is happening—it's painful! But afterward there will be a peaceful harvest of right living for those who are trained in this way.

So take a new grip with your tired hands and strengthen your weak knees. Mark out a straight path for your feet so that those who are weak and lame will not fall but become strong. (Hebrews 12:5-13)

Experiencing the negative consequences of our bad

---

59 Proverbs 3:11-12.

behavior can seem somehow unfair to us. But clearly, if God's children are offended by the severity of any punishment they suffer, their perspectives must still be somewhat skewed by feelings of self-importance.

You see, what those who sin truly *deserve* is annihilation—complete separation from a holy God. But because of God's great love toward us, we receive from Him not only the opportunity to change before further correction is applied but also the beauty of restoration once our hearts repent and are turned toward Him.

This is His boundless love displayed for us! Listen to these beautiful words from Ezekiel as God speaks restoration over His scattered children:

> *For I will gather you up from all the nations and bring you home again to your land. Then I will sprinkle clean water on you, and you will be clean. Your filth will be washed away, and you will no longer worship idols. And I will give you a new heart, and I will put a new spirit in you. I will take out your stony, stubborn heart and give you a tender, responsive heart. And I will put my Spirit in you so that you will follow my decrees and be careful to obey my regulations.* (Ezekiel 36:24-27)

How could a perfect God love such an imperfect people? But it's true. He does.

It's through understanding and confronting our own imperfections that we begin to fully realize and accept His boundless love. We actually tend to restrict our ability to receive His incredible love by our unwillingness to acknowledge the depth of our own sin. I am overcome with gratitude as I continue to read God's words through Ezekiel:

> I will cleanse you of your filthy behavior. I will give you good crops of grain, and I will send no more famines on the land. I will give you great harvests from your fruit trees and fields, and never again will the surrounding nations be able to scoff at your land for its famines. Then you will remember your past sins and despise yourselves for all the detestable things you did. But remember, says the Sovereign Lord, I am not doing this because you deserve it. O my people of Israel, you should be utterly ashamed of all you have done! (Ezekiel 36:29-32)

Unfortunately, we are inclined toward spending our energy trying to excuse our sins and cover our inadequacies, not remember them. But it is in realizing and remembering our sins that we begin to discover the depth of His love for us—especially as revealed through His Son, Jesus Christ. As we personally accept our own utter dysfunction and turn to God, His love wholly covers us.

We must turn to Him. We must acknowledge our own inability to live above sin under our own power. And we must trade our inability for His capability to empower us to live in obedience. Deciding to do these things daily positions us to receive the outpouring of His extravagant love. I wish it were easier for everyone to admit that we would all do well to completely yield ourselves to Him, but for some reason many hold on to the idea that we can successfully work our own way through life without His assistance.

I laugh a little at the thought that we can be successful in life by leaning on our own strength and goodness, because quite honestly, I've made that mistake myself. I hate to admit it, but there have been times when I've relied on my own abilities and then subsequently discovered the futility of that effort.

Of course I'm not alone in realizing that my best attempts to rely on myself are no match for His grace-filled outpouring of love. Countless men and women have found themselves at the feet of Jesus in utter humility and deep gratitude for His boundless love. As you join me there, we will find ourselves in good company.

Those who experience God's boundless love poured out upon them find themselves standing in a transformational new reality. Who they are becomes more closely defined by who *He* is, and He *is love*. And in that new realization, they can stop desperately holding on to their own limited understanding of love and willingly yield to God's love in times of brokenness.

Certainly, the Bible reveals how God sometimes demonstrates corrective love through judgment on nations. But God's love has also been shown in Scripture through many demonstrations of correction that were meted out to individuals whose lives needed to be redirected. Jonah was one of the Old Testament characters who experienced that. In the New Testament, Saul's (Paul's) conversion experience serves as an example of how God's unmitigated love is manifested through correction.

Saul found himself standing in a position of brokenness before God, whom he thought he was defending but was actually fighting against. He was faced with having to admit he was terribly wrong and needed to submit his stubborn will to God. He was faced with a choice, and his response to God would prove to be the difference between him continuing to live a vain, judgmental life or a life of love lived for Christ—and for the benefit of others.

Reading in the book of Acts, we are first introduced to Saul as we join the crowd of Jewish leaders levying their final, fatal accusations against one of the faithful leaders of the early Church, a man named Stephen.[60]

---

60 Acts 6.

But Stephen, full of the Holy Spirit, gazed steadily into heaven and saw the glory of God, and he saw Jesus standing in the place of honor at God's right hand. And he told them, "Look, I see the heavens opened and the Son of Man standing in the place of honor at God's right hand!"

Then they put their hands over their ears and began shouting. They rushed at him and dragged him out of the city and began to stone him. His accusers took off their coats and laid them at the feet of a young man named Saul.

As they stoned him, Stephen prayed, "Lord Jesus, receive my spirit." He fell to his knees, shouting, "Lord, don't charge them with this sin!" And with that, he died.

Saul was one of the witnesses, and he agreed completely with the killing of Stephen. A great wave of persecution began that day, sweeping over the church in Jerusalem; and all the believers except the apostles were scattered through the regions of Judea and Samaria.

(Acts 7:55-8:1)

Saul stood among the witnesses as a willing participant in the death of Stephen. After that, motivated by his own growing, righteous indignation, Saul began his efforts to destroy the Church. He began scouring the cities and countryside, dragging Christ-believing men and women from their homes to have them thrown them in jail.[61]

---

61 Acts 8:3.

Saul had been trained by Israel's most respected teachers of the Law. He was fully committed to the Law, and his mission was clear: pursue those heretics and keep them from causing any more trouble. Saul and other zealous religious leaders hunted down Christians to stop the spread of Christianity. But God took action and brought Saul to his point of having to decide whether to continue in the way he thought was right (but was so very wrong) or accept God's way.

As he was approaching Damascus on this mission, a light from heaven suddenly shone down around him. He fell to the ground and heard a voice saying to him, "Saul! Saul! Why are you persecuting me?"

"Who are you, lord?" Saul asked.

And the voice replied, "I am Jesus, the one you are persecuting! Now get up and go into the city, and you will be told what you must do." (Acts 9:3-6)

That was Saul's moment of truth—his opportunity to experience the overwhelming, life-changing power of God's grace-filled love through correction. Saul picked himself up off the ground and realized that he was blind. Then those who were with him led him to Damascus, where he stayed for three days without eating or drinking.

God then called upon a believer named Ananias to go to Saul and lay his hands on him so that Saul might see again. Ananias was reluctant to approach Saul, but that was certainly understandable given Saul's reputation. However, God didn't relent in appointing Ananias to the task.

> But the Lord said, "Go, for Saul is my chosen instrument to take my message to the Gentiles and to kings, as well as to the people of Israel. And I will show him how much he must suffer for my name's sake." (Acts 9:15-16)

On first reading a person who doesn't know better might think that God was about to give Saul what he deserved (*and I will show him how much he must suffer*). However, thinking that would keep a person from seeing the bigger picture of how God was demonstrating His love through Saul's experience—how God was reaching out in grace to bless even the Church's enemy.

Saul accepted God's correction, God's healing for his eyes, and God's will for his life. The Lord opened not only Saul's physical eyes but also the eyes of his understanding, and He did it through a sovereign act of love and forgiveness. As a result, Saul chose to accept and follow God's *Truth*.[62]

Saul, who became more commonly known by the Greek form of his name, Paul, indeed suffered much at the hands of

---

62 "Jesus told [Thomas], 'I am the way, the truth, and the life. No one can come to the Father except through me'" (John 14:6).

men as he went about fulfilling God's call on his life. Tasked with bringing the salvation message to the Gentiles, Paul continually endured the accusatory hatred of the Jewish religious hierarchy. Paul chose to suffer as a Christian and accept the persecution he formerly had been willing to deliver to others.

Later in Paul's ministry, he reflected on God's purposes in his life and his moment of conversion:

> *But even before I was born, God chose me and called me by*
> *his marvelous grace. Then it pleased him to reveal his Son*
> *to me so that I would proclaim the Good News about Jesus*
> *to the Gentiles.*   (Galatians 1:15-16)

It is said by some that no other person, apart from Christ, shaped the unfolding history of Christianity as much as Paul did in the days of the early Church. Through his missionary efforts and the pastoral care he provided to other leaders in the Church, the message of salvation through Christ quickly spread like a wildfire across the known world. God's kingdom was advanced by Paul, and it was all because God reached out to him with correction and grace to demonstrate His love.

We see that the boundless love of God has been revealed in Scripture through both judgment and correction in a way that is redemptive and restorative—especially when it comes to His Children. We see it in the Old Testament. We see it in the New Testament. And we see it today as God continues to deal with both nations and individuals.

God never changes. He continues to be the same Father He has always been as He lovingly but sometimes firmly corrects His children. And Peter understood that God treated all His children without favoritism.

And remember that the heavenly Father to whom you pray has no favorites. He will judge or reward you according to what you do. So you must live in reverent fear of him during your time here as "temporary residents."

(1 Peter 1:17)

God's love for His children is demonstrated through both corrections and rewards. It is up to us to either accept His love, as demonstrated, or reject it. And it is up to us to respond to the Lord's love by returning to Him the love we owe Him and by living in reverent fear and respect of His position.

What we *owe* God is reciprocal love. We need to love Him and show that we appreciate Him for who He is and what He has done for us. Jesus gave everything for us. He allowed himself to be judged for us. He died for us so we might know the true, complete, and boundless love of God.

But there is something else we must do to show our love and appreciation for what the Lord has done for us. Peter reminds us of that responsibility:

Through Christ you have come to trust in God. And you have placed your faith and hope in God because he raised Christ from the dead and gave him great glory. You were cleansed from your sins when you obeyed the truth, so now you must show sincere love to each other as brothers and sisters. Love each other deeply with all your heart.

(1 Peter 1:21-22)

If we really know, seek after, and follow God, then we have no excuse for not knowing love. And if we have experienced salvation and now understand the extent of God's love, we have no excuse for failing to exhibit that love to each other as Scripture demands. We will love others both *sincerely* and *deeply*.

Peter's letter to his fellow believers encouraged them in their suffering to know that Christ's love was being perfected in them through their experiences—even through persecution and suffering. And He made it clear that such perfected love—God's love—would be manifested through their love for one another.

So then, since Christ suffered physical pain, you must arm yourselves with the same attitude he had, and be ready to suffer, too. For if you have suffered physically for Christ, you have finished with sin. You won't spend the rest of your lives chasing your own desires, but you will be anxious to do the will of God ... Most important of all, continue to show deep love for each other, for love covers a multitude of sins. (1 Peter 4:1-2, 8)

God has a reason for any judgment He carries out against sin or any correction He provides to His children. And He also has a reason for allowing any persecution or difficult circumstances to come the way of His followers. God's love for us motivates Him to correct us when that is needed. But He is also active in revealing His love through every circumstance that comes our way.[63]

Because He is both a loving Father and Lord of our lives, God not only corrects and prepares us for life but also continues throughout our lives to teach and guide us in living and ministry. Be it through judgment, through correction, or through leading us, comforting us, and providing wisdom to us when persecution or challenges cause us suffering this side of eternity, God continues to demonstrate his love to us as He works in our lives.

Praise God for His boundless love!

---

63 "And we know that God causes everything to work together for the good of those who love God and are called according to his purpose for them" (Romans 8:28).

CHAPTER 10

Joyful Surrender

ACCORDING TO WEBSTER'S *New World Dictionary*, suffering is defined as "the bearing or undergoing of pain, distress, or injury."[64] Although our challenges in life can cause us such unwanted suffering, the words of Scripture encourage us, and they provide to us the confidence to declare that we don't have to walk through these challenges alone. With our lives surrendered to God, we not only endure suffering but also live productive, joyful lives in the face of it.

Regardless of whether our suffering is due to either emotional or physical challenges, this life will most certainly yield painful moments. But through the pain—in the midst of our troubles—we can learn to yield to our loving God the control of both our lives and the troubles we experience.

---

64 Webster's New World Dictionary, Second College Edition, 1984

That done, we can walk in joy no matter the circumstances. We can be at peace with the fact that life is made up of both joy-filled and pain-filled moments.

We tend to act surprised when we experience pain in life—since suffering is an intrusion into what we believe should be a comfortable existence. But throughout Peter's first letter to his fellow believers, he reminds them that the suffering they were experiencing was neither unexpected nor unfruitful. And at the end of his letter, Peter stated:

> *My purpose in writing is to encourage you and assure you that what you are experiencing is truly part of God's grace for you. Stand firm in this grace.* (1 Peter 5:12b)

Among other things we've dealt with in this book, we have discussed properly responding to God's correction, enduring trials, being worthy leaders, maintaining proper relationships, and maintaining hope in the face of difficulty. And this book deals with the theme of surrendering our will to God and faithfully trusting God to bring us through the suffering brought on by persecution. But there are other things that bring about suffering in this life.

Much too often it seems, physical pain, sickness, and disease touch our lives both personally and through the afflictions experienced by our loved ones. And when we experience loss, the emotional pain we suffer reminds us of not only our humanity but also the fleeting nature of the world in which we live. Although we might be tempted to feel defeated by this suffering and discouragement, we do well to continually remind ourselves of these words that Jesus spoke to His disciples:

> *Here on earth you will have many trials and sorrows. But take heart, because I have overcome the world.*
>
> (John 16:33b)

Jesus has become our greatest example of not only how to live in general but also how to deal with suffering. He suffered the pain of rejection and betrayal, and He experienced the excruciating physical pain of being beaten and dying by crucifixion. Jesus knew both emotional and physical suffering, and He overcame both.

In addition to being an example of enduring suffering, He also is our deliverer; and He has become our *High Priest.* As our High Priest, He continually presents our needs before the Father with an understanding heart. The words of Hebrews encourage us to take advantage of that knowledge and come before God's throne with the expectation that He will help us in our suffering.

> *So then, since we have a great High Priest who has entered heaven, Jesus the Son of God, let us hold firmly to what we believe. This High Priest of ours understands our weaknesses, for he faced all of the same testings we do, yet*

he did not sin. So let us come boldly to the throne of our gracious God. There we will receive his mercy, and we will find grace to help us when we need it most.

(Hebrews 4:14-16)

Just as Jesus was tested, so are His followers. Christians around the world, both past and present, have suffered various forms of persecution at the hands of those who oppose the ways of God. And they have also suffered through all the other painful and challenging things that life has to offer. But amid all that suffering, God's children have always been able to rest in knowing Jesus understands their weaknesses and has compassion on them.

The writer of Hebrews taught that in order for Jesus to qualify as our High Priest, He had to be born a man and be subject to weaknesses and suffering so He could represent us with compassion.[65] Knowing this is a great encouragement as we put our faith in the truth of Scripture. But think of Peter; he first received Christ's understanding and compassion first hand—in the flesh.

Peter's personal experience gained while walking with Jesus, and what he continued to learn through the work of the Holy Spirit in him after the day of Pentecost, allowed him to speak with confidence of God's ability to work in believers' lives for their good through every experience and

---

65 Hebrews 5:1-2; 5:8.

difficulty. With great understanding, Peter encouraged his brothers and sisters in Christ with these words:

Dear friends, don't be surprised at the fiery trials you are going through, as if something strange were happening to you. Instead, be very glad—for these trials make you partners with Christ in his suffering, so that you will have the wonderful joy of seeing his glory when it is revealed to all the world. If you are insulted because you bear the name of Christ, you will be blessed, for the glorious Spirit of God rests upon you.   (1 Peter 4:12-14)

Just as those early believers learned, we also can choose to see our trials as opportunities to partner with Christ in His suffering. Jesus came to Earth, lived as a human being, and willingly suffered the pain His life brought to Him so we could rejoice with Him both now and in eternity.

Peter's words confidently show us that we can have joy and blessing as the result of our trials. We needn't think of ourselves enduring suffering to no end. If we perceive our trials as only useless inconveniences—if we are unable to see the good God can bring from our suffering—then clearly we need to change the way we look at things.

As we set our eyes on God's purposes—on His kingdom—we are filled with hope for the future that awaits us. And with hope for the future, our trials can be seen as momentary compared to the blessed eternity we will spend with Christ.

This provides us with an eternal perspective, and this eternal perspective brings us joy and blessing in the midst of our trials.

In his letter to the church at Colosse, the apostle Paul reminded the believers there to set their minds on eternity with Christ:

> *Since you have been raised to new life with Christ, set your sights on the realities of heaven, where Christ sits in the place of honor at God's right hand. Think about the things of heaven, not the things of earth. For you died to this life, and your real life is hidden with Christ in God. And when Christ, who is your life, is revealed to the whole world, you will share in all his glory.* (Colossians 3:1-4)

Paul's words still encourage us today to focus on eternal things as we go through life. And it seems clear in Scripture that Jesus himself was able to endure His own painful suffering of being rejected, beaten, and crucified because His focus was on something eternal. His focus was on fulfilling the eternal plan of God for our salvation.

The writer of Hebrews wrote that Jesus endured the things He suffered *"because of the joy awaiting him"*—the joy He found in fulfilling the will of His father.

> *And let us run with endurance the race God has set before us. We do this by keeping our eyes on Jesus, the champion*

who initiates and perfects our faith. Because of the joy awaiting him, he endured the cross, disregarding its shame. Now he is seated in the place of honor beside God's throne. Think of all the hostility he endured from sinful people; then you won't become weary and give up. After all, you have not yet given your lives in your struggle against sin. (Hebrews 12:1b-4)

The writer of Hebrews said that Jesus "initiates and perfects our faith." It is only through His continuing work in our lives that our faith is perfected. God uses the trials in life to perfect our faith and help us mature in Christlikeness—to become like Him in character.

To be like Him we must grow in patience and selflessness. But we most likely would not grow in those ways if life were free of trials and suffering. The trials in life act as counterweights to help us build up our strength and mature in our relationship with Christ as we properly exercise our faith.

None of God's children have ever been exempt from testing. And God's use of trying circumstances to bring spiritual maturity to people is not relegated to New Testament times. God has always used His followers' difficulties, challenges, and suffering as trials and tests to shape their character.

The Old Testament patriarch, Abraham, experienced many trials; and God used each one of them to shape his character and bring him into godly maturity. The most severe test, though, was when God instructed Abraham to take his son Isaac—the son God promised him—to Mount Moriah and sacrifice him there.

But Abraham didn't question God; he simply obeyed.

The next morning Abraham got up early. He saddled his donkey and took two of his servants with him, along with his son, Isaac. Then he chopped wood for a fire for a burnt offering and set out for the place God had told him about.

(Genesis 22:3)

Abraham took his son with him to Mount Moriah. He built an altar of sacrifice there. And then he bound his son and laid him on the altar. But as Abraham lifted the knife to kill his son, the angel of the Lord called out to Abraham from heaven.

"Don't lay a hand on the boy!" the angel said. "Do not hurt him in any way, for now I know that you truly fear God. You have not withheld from me even your son, your only son."

(Genesis 22:12)

The writer of Hebrews spoke of Abraham's obedience generations later:

> *It was by faith that Abraham offered Isaac as a sacrifice*
> *when God was testing him. Abraham, who had received*
> *God's promises, was ready to sacrifice his only son, Isaac,*
> *even though God had told him, "Isaac is the son through*
> *whom your descendants will be counted."* [66] *Abraham*
> *reasoned that if Isaac died, God was able to bring him back*
> *to life again. And in a sense, Abraham did receive his son*
> *back from the dead.* (Hebrews 11:17-19)

Abraham exhibited his faith through his obedience to God. He chose to trust God rather than rely on his own understanding. And clearly, Abraham's trust in the Lord had to have increased through every challenge he faced as he demonstrated his faith in God. Through *our* testing in trials, we too progressively learn to depend less on ourselves and trust God more.

The very nature of our surrender to God is found in our ability to rise above our own understanding and yield ourselves to the leadership of God, who has power over even life and death. That is seen in Abraham's actions.

In our human nature, we're prone to hold on to a false sense of control as we go about our daily activities. And when our circumstances in life become overwhelming, we tend to exert even more effort toward controlling our own situation. But God, through His Word, encourages

---

66 Genesis 21:12.

us to do just the opposite—give up to Him our need to maintain control.

As Jesus told His disciples about His impending death, He turned to a crowd of people nearby and said, *"If any of you wants to be my follower, you must give up your own way, take up your cross daily, and follow me. If you try to hang on to your life, you will lose it. But if you give up your life for my sake, you will save it"* (Luke 9:23-24).

Our success in following Christ—our victory—is made possible by our decision to completely surrender to Christ. Our greatest satisfaction and joy in life should come from surrendering to God and resting in the wisdom, strength, and sovereignty of our Savior. The internal freedom that results from this level of surrender is truly liberating.

As we let go of our need to protect and control our own lives, we will realize that we were never meant by our Creator to be in control at all. We were meant to live under *His* control and in the peace of simply trusting in Him.

Living in complete peace, joy, and spiritual freedom under God's care begins with yielding control of our lives, our experiences, and our futures to Him.

As a working mother of three young children, my days were filled with the tasks of caring for my little ones and making sure all the daily chores were accomplished. Rising early each school-day morning, I prayed, showered, made the children's breakfast, prepared sack lunches, gathered backpacks, tied shoes, and hurried everyone toward the car.

There was a schedule that needed to be kept in order for my days to run smoothly. And it seemed all of life had been relegated to keeping that schedule. Control in my life meant staying on schedule and making sure each member of my family was doing his or her part to keep things running smoothly. I suppose somewhere along the way, maintaining the presence of God in my life became secondary to staying on task.

I remember coming to the point where I became intensely, spiritually thirsty for God's presence amid the busyness of life. One weekend, out of desperation I chose to fast and plead with God to fill the emptiness I felt inside me. As I knelt in prayer one evening, I heard His Holy Spirit deep within me ask a question.

He asked, "When are you going to give up control?"

My life had become a series of self-controlled actions, and God was calling me into the freedom of completely yielding my life to *His* control.

I remember saying in response, "God, if I give up control, I don't know who I'll be."

Having a *Type-A* personality, my life had been built around being capable, organized, and somewhat self-sufficient. And God was challenging me to completely yield my ways of living to His plan and purpose for my life.

Internally, doing what God was asking me to do—to trust that what He had for me was exponentially better than the life I had created for myself—felt a bit like walking to the edge of a cliff and simply stepping off. But because of my utter desperation, I decided to trust Him and step off that proverbial cliff.

And I'm so glad I did!

When I fully surrendered to God's will, His care, and His direction, I began to discover a freedom in Christ that I had never known. My perspective began shifting. I started to view things more from His perspective, and the joy I discovered is still increasingly uncontainable today. I wish I would have discovered this freedom and joy earlier in my life!

There is such joy and satisfaction in allowing God to lead our lives. That sense of joy and peace permeates even our most difficult moments. We're better able to endure our trials and circumstances when we trust that God will guide and lead us through them to victory. And we can maintain joy in the middle of our trials when we know that God in His sovereignty has seen the end of our trials from the beginning and will bring us through every one of them.

I have always loved Psalm twenty-three. It is a beautiful reminder that no matter the circumstances we may encounter, God lovingly leads us into His presence. In His presence is a beautiful place of victory and joyful living prepared just for us.

> The LORD is my shepherd; I have all that I need. He lets me rest in green meadows; he leads me beside peaceful streams. He renews my strength. He guides me along right paths, bringing honor to his name. Even when I walk through the darkest valley, I will not be afraid, for you are close beside me. Your rod and your staff protect and comfort me. You prepare a feast for me in the presence of my enemies. You honor me by anointing my head with oil. My cup overflows with blessings. Surely your goodness and unfailing love will pursue me all the days of my life, and I will live in the house of the LORD forever.

With our hearts fully yielded to God, we find freedom to live joyfully under our Shepherd's care. There is true joy to be found in surrendering our wills, our difficulties, our fears, and our futures to our heavenly Father!

Peter, like so many who lived before him, and like so many who have lived since, learned what it means to surrender everything to God. He surrendered his pride to God. He surrendered his failures to God. He surrendered his weaknesses to God. He surrendered his strengths to God. He surrendered his past to God. And he surrendered all of his future to God in order to better know Him and become everything God wanted him to be.

Peter wanted others to know God the way he knew Him. He wanted others to know God's desires for them, and he wanted them to know and experience the same joy he had found in trusting and following Christ. So inspired by the Holy Spirit, Peter took the time to put his thoughts down in a letter, and he sent it to those who needed the instruction and reassurance he had to offer them. Written from a heart fully surrendered to God, Peter's inspired words of encouragement continue to bless us today.

Peter didn't just know *about* Jesus; he walked alongside Him for three years. Time spent with Jesus had changed him. He knew first-hand the forgiveness and hope that Jesus brought to his life. And Peter knew as well as anyone what it was like to live a life in joyful surrender to God. He knew all the benefits of that.

And now, so do I.